Thirty-Two Words for Field

Lost words of the Irish landscape

Manchán Magan

Gill Books

Gill Books
Hume Avenue
Park West
Dublin 12
www.gillbooks.ie

Gill Books is an imprint of M.H. Gill and Co.
© Manchán Magan 2020

978 07171 87973

Edited by Ruairí Ó Brógáin
Proofread by Neil Burkey
Illustrations by Steve Doogan
Printed by CPI Group (UK) Ltd, Croydon, CRO 4YY
This book is typeset in 14 on 22pt, Adobe Garamond

A CIP catalogue record for this book is
available from the British Library.
15 14 13 12 11

MIX
Paper from
responsible sources
FSC   FSC® C171272
www.fsc.org

CONTENTS

Breifne, a tiny hole made by an insect or a needle, has its direct opposite in *duibheachán*, a hole so big that it can be classed as an abyss. *Pluais*, *séib*, *sloc*, *cluais* and *logán* are all other possibilities, some more specific than others.

Each can be translated into the English word 'hole', and perhaps it's efficient to do so, but I have always wondered what subtlety and nuance is lost and whether the richness of the reality the Irish words describe would wane.

Our landscape now looks like an increasingly anonymous expanse of indistinguishable fields, yet seen through the Irish language each field has its own word, depending on its characteristics and function: *geamhar, bánóg, biorrach, machaire, buaile, ingealtas, domasach, póicín, fásach, mainnear, cathairín, réidh, cuibhreann, réidhleán, cluain, mín, tamhnach, buadán, tuar, branar, plás, raon, lóiste, cúilín, réalóg, cabhán, achadh, mothar, plásóg, loscán, páirc, magh.* To a city-dweller this land may all look the same, and in English each would probably be just referred to as a field, yet to someone whose ancestors have been cultivating the land, growing grain and tending cattle for over four thousand years, and who has built up the soil over centuries by hauling seaweed from the shore and burning limestone to add alkalinity, they look very different.

Geamhar is a field of corn grass, *biorrach* is a marshy field, *branar* is a fallow field. *Cuibhreann* is a tilled field worked in partnership with a neighbour, *tuar* a night field for cattle. *Cluain* is a meadow field between two woods, *tamhnach* an arable field in an arid area. *Réidhleán* is a field for games or dancing, *plás* a level field for spreading flax or hay, *plásóg* a sheltered field in which a mare would foal, *raon* an upland field, *machaire* a low-lying open field. *Buaile* is a field for keeping cattle before milking. *Mainnear* is an enclosed field, *réidh* a level field, *mín* a smooth fine field and *réalóg* an unenclosed patch of good land in the middle of a *créig* (a stonier area of limestone). *Cathairín* is a field with a fairy-dwelling in it. *Losaid*, a neat, well-arranged field, is similar to *cúilín*, which is also neat but smaller.

Each of these words summons particular swathes of our landscape and the activities that happen on them. Some words even refer to fields in which something occasionally happened but no longer does, such as *bánóg*, a patch of ground levelled out by years of dancing, among other things, or *buadán*, a hillside that once had gorse growing on it but has since been cut with a scythe or hook, leaving only stumps. A hillside on which the gorse has been removed not by cutting but by burning is a *loscán*.

Having lived here for so long, we have perhaps inevitably become rooted to every aspect of this land, becoming entangled in its complex network of clay, sand, stone, weeds, worms, mycobacteria, flora, pollinators and mycelium. But I hadn't realised how far back this connection stretched until my grandmother taught me a *seanfhocal* (a proverb, literally 'old word') that shook my sense of time and space so much that I am contending with it to this day.

Saol trí mhíol mhór saol iomaire amháin, saol trí iomaire saol an domhain.

These words – meaning 'Three times the life of a whale is the lifespan of a ridge, and three times the life of a ridge is the lifespan of the world' – encapsulate just how far back the knowledge contained within the language stretches on this island. A whale was thought to live for one thousand years (although they live for about a century), so it was known that the cultivation ridges that we see in the fields around us could be up to three thousand years old. Archaeologists agree that there are indeed ridges of that age still visible in such places as the Céide Fields in Co. Mayo and Slievemore on Achill Island. The span of three cultivation ridges would amount to nine thousand years, which takes us back to the time when archaeologists believe significant numbers of humans first settled here – the beginning of our world. That our people appear to have kept a count of how long we have been here – and that they encoded it in our language – is precious.

My grandmother often pointed out the still-visible cultivation ridges left by her great-grandparents' generation during the Famine in the 1840s. Some were more visible than others, as they had been left undug; my ancestors either were too weak to dig them or, having noticed the blight-rotted potato stems, had realised that there would be nothing but a slimy mush beneath the soil. I had been struck by the longevity of such memories, but it wasn't until I heard the proverb that I realised quite how far back these folk memories stretch.

It appears, at least, as though we managed to keep some wispy thread of memory intact from our Neolithic forebears, who planted, weeded and harvested along such ridges thousands of years ago. The knowledge is contained within the land, and over the years I've realised that the best way to access it is through the language.

FIRST UTTERANCE

Aduantas is that feeling one gets in unfamiliar places – a light fear with a tinge of sadness. It captures well the sense of, say, starting out on a book on something as potent and amorphous as the Irish language. This feeling is mixed with a sense of *sclimpíní*, which conveys the effect of lights dancing before one's eyes – either real light or supernatural light, those glimpses one gets through the veil of what lies beyond.

When the forebears of those Neolithic farmers first arrived on this island ten thousand years ago, they didn't yet speak Irish, but that doesn't mean we don't know what was first said. The unfathomable process known as the oral tradition has left us a record, passed down through the generations in the minds of druids and poets until the arrival of that poisoned chalice – writing – in the fifth century with the first missionaries, who used it as a spell to entrance us and as a tool to control us.

It was they who helped jot down and then transcribe our first memories, insights and acts onto parchment, and from there these have made their way to us in the form of a shabby set of ancient tweets, known as annals and chronicles, that list the history of our people from the time of Noah's flood to our arrival on this green island and right up to the 17th century.

The annals were like newspaper headlines, noting the most significant events, such as that 'a huge dragon was seen, with great thunder after it, at the end of autumn' in AD 736 and that 'ships with their crews were seen in the air above Cluain Moccu Nóis' in AD 749. We also know that in AD 1116 there was a 'great famine in the spring, so that a man would sell his son and his daughter for food and men would even eat one another, and dogs.'

It is these written records that claim that we first set foot here on 1 April in 700 BC, having sailed from Spain. Many archaeologists agree with this account but suggest that the date is closer to 8000 BC ... Both versions may be right in different ways.

The old lore also preserves the first words spoken here. They were an invocation by our chief poet and druid, Amergin, who, it is said, managed to reach the coast of Co. Kerry because of a magical wave that plucked him from the Atlantic Ocean and dropped him on the shore during a tempest. His wife and his siblings were all drowned in this storm that was created by a supernatural tribe of earth-bound gods, Tuatha Dé Danann, who were living here before us. They had made a promise that if we managed to reach Ireland from a distance of nine waves from the shore they would gladly surrender.

When Amergin did make it to dry land in spite of the storm they had sent, they fulfilled their promise and slunk away under the surface of the earth into the Otherworld, where they continued to live.

Amergin became leader of the island and his first act was to begin uttering an incantation, summoning up the world that we intended to create here and clarifying the interrelation between it and all other planes of existence, physical and spiritual.

This could be seen as a rather obtuse thing to do, but the Irish people always had a flair for the dramatic. Proclamations, blessings and invocations are second nature to us; often, we favour them over actions. And yet Amergin's words were somewhat different; they were our declaration of the unity of all things, and our lives have been based on it ever since.

Am gaeth i m-muir	I am wind on sea
Am tond trethan	I am ocean wave
Am fuaim mara	I am roar of sea
Am dam secht ndirend	I am stag of seven tines
Am séig i n-aill	I am hawk on cliff

Am dér gréne	I am shining tear of sun
Am cain lubai …	I am gentle herbs …

His incantation continues for many lines, laying out who we are in this world and beyond, making it clear that we are all things, united as one entity beyond the veil of duality.

When I was young I recited these words, hoping to get to grips with them. The Irish in them is very old and has an incantatory quality, as if the sounds were designed as much to summon the object into this realm as to describe it.

In a way, everything that I want to say in this book is contained within those lines. They reveal a language that not only describes things but also summons them into being, a language that communicates not only to others but to the psyche and the subconscious, a language that is deeply rooted in the environment and can connect us to our surroundings in remarkable ways.

Amergin's words, just like the Irish language itself, are our gift to ourselves from the ancient past, grounding us to this particular emerald patch while also hinting that we are connected to everywhere else, reminding us that we are united and connected to all things – waves, fields, hawks.

ISN'T IT YOURSELF?

When I was young, locals in the West Kerry *Gaeltacht* where I spent four months of each year would greet me with *Nach tú?* ('Isn't it yourself?'), and I'd answer *Is mé* ('It's me'), though I was never all that certain who I was. I envied the locals their sense of certainty.

They had been brought up in the Irish language on a rocky, mountainous peninsula protruding into the Atlantic, not far from where the druid Amergin first landed, whereas I spent only a quarter of each year there, spending the rest of my time living in the polar opposite world of the *Galltacht* ('foreign-speaking realm') – an affluent suburb of Dublin – attending a private school and playing with children who had no knowledge of, or interest in, Irish. In Co. Kerry I'd go to the Irish-speaking national school with the children of fishermen and farmers (and when I say 'farmers' I mean men who cared for no more than a dozen cows and who had a few hens, some ridges of vegetables and fields of hay).

During those four months, I'd be gathering water from the well, seaweed from the shore, milk from the farm and mushrooms from the fields – all through Irish. I'd help save the hay, load milk churns on the pony cart or eavesdrop on old men around the anvil at the forge. I learnt then that the block of wood over which the blacksmith worked was a *ceap*, which also means 'tree stump', because long ago they hammered a tree trunk deep into the ground to provide a sturdy base for the anvil. The word *ceap* came to mean the place one felt most rooted, where one was secure and nurtured. From there it developed into meaning a nursery bed for plants, the stock of a wheel and the head of a tribe or family.

In Dublin there was no possible use for a word like *ceap* or for words like *sopóg* (a torch made of straw, rushes or bog deal mounted on a pole and used by river poachers) and *ruaimneach* (the hair from a horse's tail used in rope). I spoke only English in Dublin and did what other city children in the seventies did: built Airfix planes, played with Meccano and Lego and bought Marvel comics and Bazooka bubble-gum with my pocket money. I dressed in the latest sweatshirts and jeans, with puffer jackets and the plastic sun visors clad in towelling cloth that we saw on 'The Brady Bunch' and that were worn by John McEnroe at Wimbledon.

I had no real *cranna foirtil*, which is akin to *ceap* but refers in particular to strong branches or stout oars that form the support poles to help guide us through life. The closest thing I had was BBC children's television and the few films that preoccupied my imagination: *Star Wars*, *Jaws* and *ET*. It was these that helped make sense of my Dublin world, but they had no relevance to my other existence in Co. Kerry.

When in the Gaeltacht I'd often head up to the pier in Baile na nGall with my brother to spend time with the old men as they watched their sons fixing and folding nets, baiting lobster pots and going out to sea in *naomhóga*, the same frail wooden boats that Amergin himself had arrived on (though these boats were now clad in tar and canvas instead of cow hide). The local people found our slight foreignness amusing and would allow us to linger and listen, sending us to the shops for tobacco or matches, with extra pennies to buy a lollipop.

I would watch them closely, envying the certitude of their existence, the confidence with which they could answer *Is mé* to that existential question *Nach tú?* I wanted that same certainty. I imagined it was similar to Amergin's as he proclaimed himself the roar of the sea, the hawk on a cliff, the sparkling sun. But I was always aware that Baile na nGall meant 'townland of the foreigners', which is what I was, a *gall*, or foreigner, with a foot in both worlds – or neither.

Many of us feel similar, sensing that we are connected to an ancient ancestral language and an elemental, place-based culture but finding it hard to define what that means. We know there must have been a good reason for our people to have buried a horse's skull in the floor, to have placed a cow's hocks up the chimney or to have made sure to eat three good feeds of nettles in May, but we are no longer quite certain. This feeling is particularly strong among the eighty million people of Irish descent around the world, many of whom have been raised with an awareness that their culture connects them to something deep and profound – but what exactly is it?

STONES AND LOSS

We should begin at the foundations, I suppose: the rocks and stones that make up this craggy island. *Carraig* means 'rock' and *cloch* 'stone'; but, just as with fields and holes, there's a wild diversity of words to differentiate them.

Ailce is a large immovable stone, *méaróg* a finger-stone, *rothlóir* a rollable stone, *iolchloch* a stone of several virtues, *baisleac* a flat stone beside a well or stream on which women wash and beetle clothes. *Spiacán* is a sharp stone, *púntán* a round heavy stone, *spiothóg* a little stone, *líogar* a flat light stone for casting, *sail* a stone used as a shelf, *gallán* a pillar stone (supposed to be thrown by giants from the hills), *cailleach* a stone used as an anchor.

There's also *lindéar*, a large stone or rock; *anscuiche*, immovable rocks; and *boilg*, a submerged rock near the shore. *Slinn* is a flat stone; *liag* is also a flat stone but one used as a flagstone. *Lia* is a great or symbolic stone, *liagán* a hand stone. *Léag* is a precious stone or jewel, and *lóghmhar* is also a precious stone.

I could go on, but perhaps the point is not how these words show the diversity of stones or the wealth of Irish but how they show its losses. Most of these words are no longer known or at least are familiar only to the elderly. Each day more go missing.

That *bláith-liag* means a smooth stone, *foir-neach* a rolling stone and *dornóg* a small casting stone may be recorded on this page for the last time. The thought of it makes me want to keep listing words, but I know this can't help stall the inevitable process of erosion.

No book can be an archive, yet I want to have it recorded that *caid* is a binding stone, *bóic* a stone at the back of a hearth, *bannaí* a stone used as a cross bond in a wall, *spalla* a stone in a wall, *ailcid* a strand stone used in seine fishing. *Lomán* is a rock of which only the summit is exposed. *Cabhas* are stepping stones across a stream, and *carra* are stones across a causeway. *Clochrán* are stones across a ford, and a large stone can be referred to as a *béillic*, *garbhóg* or *carball*.

Most of these words were still in use in the 1970s. But now more than three-quarters are likely gone, and with them has gone all their subtleties, such as that a *méaróg* can also mean a thin hay rope made by one person and coiled up as it is being made. *Carball* can mean the roof of a dog's mouth, used to gauge its fighting ability. *Béillic* also means a cavern under a great stone and *púntán* can mean the plug in the lower of two millstones.

They are, of course, only words and, like all things, will naturally founder and fade. The optimistic side of me realises that a language is a process, and processes can be eternal. Yet with barely 80,000 speakers left, Irish is losing its body mass at a dizzying rate. It's becoming scrawny and is being confined to ever narrower geographical areas and social contexts. Its fate appears bound to follow that of other traditional customs and practices, such as dowries, dowsing and seal killing.

And yet I'm not ready to give up on such words as *reanga*, a long sharp-backed stone or rock; *scealp*, a large thin rock; *sceir*, a sharp sea rock; *speilg*, a pointed rock; *splinnc*, a high, projecting, pointing rock (usually over a precipice); *siorra*, a sharp rock rising nearly to the sea's surface; and *scor*, a rock concealed by the sea.

It's neither possible nor desirable to hang on to every venerable remnant of the past, for even stones erode. Such stones are transitory lumps of rotting sea creatures or mineral particles that gradually clump tightly together under geological pressure before eroding again over an even longer duration. Languages move at greater speed, but they too peter out, and since Irish has thrived for up to three thousand years, it has had a greater innings than most.

It might be time to cut the ties and focus on something else, but first we should consider whether languages that have clung on long enough to see rivers come and go, and rocks erode back to sand, might be equipped to express ideas otherwise impossible to express.

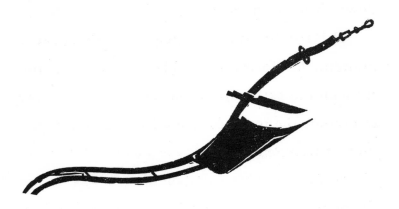

WHO ARE YOU OF?

I n Connemara, north along the coastline from Co. Kerry, local people don't ask you to vouch for your existential beingness as they do in the south. Rather than asking *Nach tú?* ('Isn't it yourself?'), they ask *Cé dhár díobh thú?* ('Who are you of?'), and it's up to the speaker to position themselves in the world in a manner that makes sense to the questioner. If, for example, you were to pose me that question, I would say that I am a descendant of Aodhagán Ó Rathaille, the last Gaelic poet to have attended the ancient bardic schools of Killarney, where the potent primacy of language was passed down through the eons.

Ó Rathaille was my great-great-great-great-granduncle. Born into poverty in 1670, he rose through the patronage of the Viscounts Kenmare to become the most learned *ollamh* (a poet of the highest rank, entitled to wear a cloak of crimson bird feathers) of his generation in a period that saw the demise of the ancient Gaelic world. For him this time marked the end of civilisation.

The *aisling* is the art form he is most associated with. It is a poetic genre in which Ireland manifests itself in the form of a woman to whom the poet succumbs, and the poet expresses yearning to her. In these works Ó Rathaille principally expresses his yearning for a return to cultural sophistication in Ireland.

Beyond the *aisling* his focus was on the *aoir*, a form of satire that was considered enormously potent and was greatly feared for the devastation it could wreak on reputations. These satires were incantatory, like Amergin's declaration, and a good *aoir* could raise a *fearb* (a weal or welt arising from satire or disgrace) on the face of its target. *Fearb* is also a blotch or a hole in a sacred parchment, maybe because these too were considered punishments for amoral actions.

The *aisling* and the *aoir* are remnants of druidic charms and spells; the latter is a direct descendant of the magical curses that druids uttered. Ó Rathaille's satires were mostly directed at the English settlers who stole Irish farms and imposed what he considered to be their boorish, exploitative ways on the land.

He is too far distant for me to feel strong kinship with, but his great-great-grandnephew Michael O'Rahilly (who called himself 'The O'Rahilly') had a direct and visceral impact on everything I am. It was he who first brought my grandmother and the rest of the family down to West Kerry in 1912 to immerse themselves in Irish, and he is how I came to speak Irish before I learnt English. He was a founder of the Irish Volunteers, the organisation that led the Easter Rising, and he was aide-de-camp to the commander-in-chief, Patrick Pearse, in the GPO in Dublin. He was later appointed military commander of the garrison when James Connolly was too injured to lead.

The Irish word for 'family' is *teaghlach*, which also means 'hearth' or 'fireside', because in an era before electricity and oil the family was dependent on the burning fire at its hearth. The O'Rahilly considered himself the head of our *teaghlach* (which is why he gave himself the honorific title 'The'), but he was also the burning ember that inspired us all. His death on the final day of the Rising of 1916, when he was riddled with bullets while leading a charge on a British machine-gun post during the evacuation of the GPO, became the catalyst for so much of what happened to my family in the 20th century.

Teaghlach can also mean 'monastic kinsmen', and in some ways The O'Rahilly was like our martyred abbot and we were his lay followers. I was taught Irish in his memory. My grandmother

Sighle Humphreys, a republican revolutionary, was 17 when she watched this man, her uncle, pulling on his fine officer's boots and strapping on his silver sword as he prepared to head out to the GPO to face probable death.

Watching him bid a final farewell to his pregnant wife and his four children, knowing that as a commanding officer he might never return, was the decisive moment in her life. For her it was the ultimate *tabharthas* ('offering' or 'sacrifice'). (*Íobairt* is now the more common word for 'sacrifice', but it has religious connotations.) *Tabharthas* conveys the idea of a sacred gift from the gods or of an offering that has unpredictable consequences, as in the old fable 'An Tabharthas a Thug Feoras go hOileán Baoi', which relates the story of a gift of a fox that transforms Dursey Island in Co. Cork.

The idealism embodied by The O'Rahilly's self-sacrifice unbalanced us all, not least his wife, a wealthy American heiress who was left to raise his five sons. I never met her, but her sons, together with my grandmother, were key figures in my childhood.

There is a word in Irish to convey the act of offering oneself as a sacrifice: *foráil*. It also means a superabundance of something, as in *foráil seirce*, 'excess of love'. And it was The O'Rahilly's excess of love, or *tírghrá* ('love of country'), that so disoriented us. *Foráil* can also mean the groove in the head of a spindle that allows the thread run generously through it, and it's as if The O'Rahilly allowed too much thread through, entangling us all.

On the day I was born – 54 years after Easter Monday, 1916 – my grandmother was still snagged in the consequences of his act (and, as I write this, 49 years after I was born, I am still quite tangled in it). I was the child of her only surviving child, and so for her I became a direct offshoot of his actions and was duty-bound to continue his legacy. She set about instilling in me the selflessness, grit and *tírghrá* she associated with him. My siblings and I were putty to be moulded in his image. Every word of Irish we spoke was both an honorific token in his memory and a bullet aimed at those in Westminster who had caused his death.

I lapped up all this heroism when I was young, wallowing in the details of his last decade on earth, during which time he had immersed himself to a fanatical degree in the revival of the Irish language and the fight for independence, developing new forms of Gaelic script, editing Irish-language newspapers and helping to guide and govern the Gaelic League, which spearheaded the revival of Irish in the late 19th and early 20th centuries. He then turned his attention to politics, becoming a founding member of the Irish Volunteers in 1913. He was appointed its Director of Arms and oversaw the purchase and importation of the rifles and ammunition that would be used in the fight for independence.

Another word for family is *treabh* (though it's more often spelt *treibh* nowadays). This word also means ploughing, tilling and striving forth, because that is what families do. The O'Rahilly was our chief *treabhach*, our ploughman, leaving behind him a powerful *treabhchas*, which means a clan or the feats they achieve.

NETHERWORLD

The O'Rahilly is long gone. W.B. Yeats described him as a man who 'had such little sense' in his poem '*The O'Rahilly*', and appears to mock him in the final line, 'How goes the weather?' a translation of 'Lá breá?', the clichéd call said to have been used by Irish language learners in the Gaeltacht when trying out their few words on locals.

The O'Rahilly may be well rotted in the soil by now but aspects of him linger, like a phantom presence. The sense I have is that he's here but not here; he's in the *alltar* and not the *ceantar*. *Ceantar* means place, region or locality, while *alltar* is its opposite: the other realm, the netherworld. In the Irish mindset the *ceantar* is closely shadowed by the *alltar*. They exist simultaneously, in all places, at all times. Our physical bodies occupy the *ceantar* but our minds can easily slip into the *alltar*.

This idea that there were different levels beneath and between what we could see was once so widely accepted that it didn't even deserve mentioning, but nowadays the word *alltar* has almost disappeared. Only a thin veil separated the two realms, *ceantar* and *alltar*, and there were always those who could pass from one to the other.

The word *púicín*, for example, means a supernatural covering that allows otherworldly beings to appear unseen in this reality. It can also mean a blindfold, goat muzzle or tin shade placed over a thieving cow's eyes. This is an example of modern languages losing something that was innate to older ones.

Irish is a language that developed before humankind decided to limit reality to the parameters of the rational mind – to believe only in a corporeal existence – and it has managed to hold on to some essential attributes of life that we risk overlooking or even forgetting in our civilised and technologically sophisticated lives.

The adjective *comhalta*, related to the word *púicín*, means 'covered' or 'hooded' but can also refer to the act of being invisible beneath magic robes, as in *comhalta faoi bhrat sí* ('hidden by a fairy mantle'). *Comhla* is an associated word meaning a leaf of a door or a gate but also a threshold to the Otherworld, as in *comhla bhreac*, a magic door to supernatural dwellings in rocks on a hillside or ring fort.

It is hard for us now to conceive of a world with such easy access to other realms, and it is also hard to imagine the consequences that arise from this. Having different realities bleeding into your own has profound repercussions on your state of mind and your thought process. And now, as we lose the ability to find this magic that has always underlain all things, we narrow our perspective from the infinite to the claustrophobic parameters of what is known and prescribed. We risk forgetting the virtues of allowing in the unknown, of acknowledging all that we do not understand, of living more uncertain but freer and more impassioned lives.

Scim is a word that links reality to the world beyond in a gritty and visceral way. Its basic meaning is a thin coating of tiny particles, like limewash on a house or dust on a mantelpiece, but it can also mean a fairy film that covers the land, or a magical vision, or succumbing to the supernatural world through sleep.

These notions seem to be vestiges of a simpler age, and yet the current frontiers of physics are proposing a theory of the universe that is eerily similar. Leaving behind a reality that was based firmly on the molecular interactions between electrons, physicists have now come to realise that electrons don't exist – or at least not as we imagined them – in one place. They are quantum, forever materialising and dematerialising and reappearing somewhere else.

So everything we think we see is not as it seems. Our bodies, fields, mountains and stars are elementary particles, vibrating and fluctuating constantly between existence and non-existence — swarming in space, even when it seems that nothing is there. They stretch out everywhere (and nowhere), combining to infinity, like the letters of a cosmic alphabet, creating the language of asteroids, cuttle-fish, chocolate, goats and galaxies.

The word that brings this home to me most clearly is *crithir*, which means a particle or spark of flame or light, or the tiniest portion of some-thing. It can also refer to the vulnerability and insubstantiality of solid objects, such as a swamp or the trembling of the land in an earthquake, or the crumbling surface of ploughed land when dry after rain. *Crithir* means all these things. And when a sheep suddenly turns slack and wobbly it is said to suffer from *crithir fola* ('trembling of the blood'), which is the Irish term for braxy, a fatal disease that arises from eating frosted root crops or grasses.

That any solid, dependable mass that starts to quiver or falter can be referred to as *crithir* makes it an ideal term for our new understanding of electrons – these particles that we have delineated as the building blocks of all life but that in fact are wholly undependable. They vanish on a whim, seemingly spontaneously, even though the whole process must be sparked by an unfathomable network that is not yet perceptible to us nor even comprehensible.

The notion is bamboozling though less so to someone comfortable with the idea that *púicín* can mean both an invisibility cloak and a goat muzzle. Long ago we seemed to know instinctively that life wasn't as it seemed. Our reality was a world of happenings, not of things.

For example, *leasú* now refers to fertiliser, an amendment or a food preserver, but it used to mean something quite different – the many activities surrounding such things – in the knowledge that fertilisation, amending and preserving are multifaceted processes that are more complex than a simple thing or act. Fortunately, *leasú* manages to preserve many of its original meanings, such as to improve, educate and repair and to tan hides and cure bacon; it is also the technical word for chemical fertiliser and the word for a political reform and for welfare. Accordingly, the Irish for 'an amendment to the welfare reform act' is *leasú an acht leasaithe leasa* – a prime example of the malleability of a single word. One further meaning of *leasú* is a point welded onto a plough iron when worn ... in case the need for such a term ever rearises. (I feel it might.)

Though I've given two meanings for *púicín*, neither is its core meaning, which is a type of dark, cramped space – somewhere that feels fuggy and fetid. It can mean a tiny hut with a single opening for sheltering geese, lambs or kids, or a dark, impoverished house. *Púicín gaoithe* refers to a magical nocturnal bird that swoops down disconcertingly, such as an owl or windhover, although it can also mean a kestrel.

The word derives from *púca*, which is entirely indefinable, being as far from a 'thing' as one can imagine. A *púca* is an energetic manifestation that engenders fear in the dark or an apparition arising from the uncertainty sparked by the absence of light. The most specific description I've found in a dictionary is an indefinitely shaped evil spirit that goes about on all fours and carries victims off on its back.

CONTORTIONS
AND COMETS

S earch for the English words 'contortion' or 'distorting' in an Irish dictionary and you'll get *riastradh*. *Fuaim riastartha* refers to distorted sound in broadcasting. *Ceol teolaí ach deas riastartha* ('music that is cosy but nicely distorted') is how the techno-funk album Throwback by the Berlin-based DJ and record producer Glenn Astro is described by Ben Ó Faoláin in the online journal Nós, while the desert-blues music of Tinariwen is categorised as *fuaim chrancrach, riastartha* ('knotted, contorted sound').

Riastradh, though, means these things only in a metaphorical way. Its real meaning is as a descriptive term for the battle spasms of Cú Chulainn, the mythical hero of the Ulster Cycle sagas. When confronted with a seemingly unbeatable obstacle his body metamorphoses in outlandish convulsions, like the battle frenzies that strike Norse warriors and a few other Irish heroes whose bones were said to twist behind and before them, allowing them to attack on all sides at once.

Yet Cú Chulainn's *riastradh* was more intense than any normal frenzy. 'The frontal sinews of his head were dragged to the back of his neck, where they showed in lumps bigger than the head of a man-child aged one month.' This is how it is described in the epic saga Táin Bó Cuailnge ('The Cattle Raid of Cooley') as translated by Eleanor Hull in 1898. It goes on: 'One eye became engulfed in his head so far that 'tis a question whether a wild heron could have got at it where it lay against his occiput, to drag it out upon the surface of his cheek; the other eye on the contrary, protruded suddenly, and of itself so rested upon the cheek.'

It reads like something from one of the more drug-inspired passages of William S. Burroughs or Irvine Welsh, and this may not be by coincidence. Some academics argue that the fly agaric mushroom played a crucial role in inducing the *riastradh*. It offered a dependable way of channelling the mindless fury of the deities of war – Morrigan, Badb and Nemain – through a hallucinogenic trance.

Certain passages in the Táin describe Cú Chulainn's mouth as twisting up to his ears while his heart beats like 'the howl of a ban-dog doing his office, or of a lion in the act of charging bears.' It does seem as if something beyond mere battle drama is being conveyed. According to the scholar Daithí Ó hÓgáin, the *riastradh* is a remnant of an enigmatic process that warriors underwent to access inspiration and strength.

The word itself is thought to derive from *re is tar*, meaning 'back and front' in Old Irish. It was a way of describing Cú Chulainn's ability to swing a sword in all directions, smiting enemies on all sides.

Nowadays the word is not so often used, but when it is, as in the music reviews noted above, all its echoes and resonances come with it. It has these live strands running back through the millennia that are palpable and visceral to those tuned in to them. A learner finding the word in a dictionary may have no sense of the multilayered package of ideas and visions that trail back through thousands of years like the ion tail of a speeding meteor, but they still exist within the word.

Neural linguistic research has shown that when we say the word 'yacht', for example, an image of one flashes before our eyes. So when a learner of Irish says the word *riastradh*, what image comes to mind? Does Cú Chulainn appear even for a split second, 'like a tree standing in a swollen stream' with 'every limb and joint trembling like a bulrush in mid-torrent'? When I hear it I think I can see a transient flash of the warrior, with 'his lion's gnash-ings causing flakes of fire, each one larger than fleece of three-year-old wether, to stream from his throat into his mouth and so outwards.'

A final facet of the word is its cosmic or meteoric element. A key part of Cú Chulainn's *riastradh* is a jet of blood that spouts from his head, forming 'a magic mist of gloom' that covered the whole sky. Professor Mike Baillie of Queen's University, Belfast, has suggested that this sounds suspiciously like a comet. The account of the *riastradh* continues: 'Taller, thicker, more rigid, longer than the mast of a great ship was the perpendicular jet of dusky blood which out of his scalp's very central point shot upwards and then was scattered to the four cardinal points.'

It sounds remarkably like a firework or a meteor shard burning through the atmosphere. It must have been a very large or slow-moving one, as it 'showed longer than the whet-stone of a first-rate man-at-arms.'

This description led Baillie to think of a comet and he has suggested that these fireworks, which arose from Cú Chulainn in 'virulent pouring showers and sparks of ruddy fire which the seething of his savage wrath caused to mount up above him', might approximate celestial displays of a comet passing the Earth close enough to penetrate its magnetosphere. He then calculated the return times of Comet Encke, which happen to synchronise with the main events in Cú Chulainn's life, around the ages of 4, 7, 14 and 17.

Comet Encke has several associated meteor showers, which would further light up the sky with moments of divine apparition. In fact scientists have often suggested that the appearance of the comet from head on, with its curved jets shooting outwards like a pinwheel, is reminiscent of the swastika shape recorded as an ancient astronomical supernatural symbol from the heavens in Chinese and Indian cultures.

Certainly comets were known to inspire awe among primitive communities all over the world, and the description of Cú Chulainn as 'a shining source of light too bright in its blinding brilliance for men to look at' is suggestive of one, particularly his swastika-like 'three distinct heads of hair' and his ability to change shape, which brings to mind the shifting forms of nebulous, burning vapour and dust seen in a comet's coma (the ring or halo effect that appears to surround it). Pliny the Elder, writing in AD 78, referred to 'a white comet with silver hair, so brilliant that it could not be looked at, and having the shape of a deity in human form.'

So, tracing the word *riastradh* to the distortion of the night's sky caused by passing galactic debris makes its use in Modern Irish so apt, whether to describe the contorted funk of a desert-blues band or, indeed, to describe the reality of contending with a language three millennia old that has developed many layers and dimensions.

LOSING A WORD

Words like *riastradh* reveal that Irish is a contin-uation and survival of an ancient way of thinking, and such words are not simply the debris of outdated beliefs, as some self-loathing critics will claim. Words like *púicín* and *alltar* underline this fact. Beneath the language's seemingly disordered patterns and patchwork is a silent substratum of folk thought, which serves to maintain an unbroken link with its roots, from which arise our most fundamental systems of thought.

Can the language help make sense of who we are? Not just sense of the current population of this island but of all humanity – of those who evolved skills and higher consciousness over millennia and spread out northwards from Africa. For what is perhaps most valuable about Irish is its direct link with the original Indo-European language, which gradually spread out from the region where humankind first settled and learnt to farm on the borderlands of Europe and Asia.

This concept is not merely poetic or sentimental but reflects the simple truth that languages offer a connection to the inner lives of our ancestors. Old ways of thinking and living remain encoded within them.

Take the Irish word *lóipín*, for example, which means the cloth fixed on a hen's claws to stop it scratching the earth. It also means pieces of jute placed on a donkey's hooves to keep them from slipping on frost. It can also mean a flake or any crude, defective thing. It brings with it many concepts and ways of seeing the world, concerning our empathy

with animals, our connection to the environment
and the things we choose to do with the time we
have at our disposal.

I haven't heard the word *lóipín* since my childhood and wouldn't be surprised if it has disappeared,
like so many of the words I heard growing up.
Except, of course, that nothing ever truly disap-
pears: the hen's claw or a snowflake decompose and
are recycled into the environment, just as the files
you delete from your computer are released into
the atmosphere as a quantity of energy that will be
absorbed by the molecules around it.

I'm curious about where all the lost words have
gone. Are they now just the sum of the resonances
and traces they have left in our minds and our landscape and culture, or do they have an afterlife of
their own? Do they leave a hole in our psyche and,
if so, what is the word for that type of hole?

Each word that has ever been uttered leaves a
traceable mark on the universe. It radiates outwards
through the air to a point where it is no longer
audible to humans, but still it continues, radiating

ever fainter through the stratosphere and beyond
as infrasound, a million billion times below our
hearing range. Each past utterance of a word may
now be oscillating only once every 10 million years,
as opposed to 20 times per second when it was first
said, but it's still there.

Old words also exist in a more tangible sense
in dictionaries – these lexicological black holes
whose mass depends on the quantity of matter
they swallow. *Lóipín* is listed there between *loinnir*
(brightness, radiance, the shimmer of the sea) and
loirg-bheart (a leg harness), though how long it will
remain there is uncertain: Irish dictionaries tend to
cull words at a brutal rate. A dictionary from the
1920s lists *lóipín* as also meaning vampless stock-
ings and an animal or bird with white legs. More
recent dictionaries make no mention of this.

Scim has also suffered this form of evisceration
in modern dictionaries, which still list its meaning
as particles of dust, limewash and similar but make
no reference to a fairy film that covers the land or
to succumbing to the supernatural world through

sleep. These are now unofficial meanings passed down by others or stumbled on while rummaging through old books.

Loirg-bheart has fared even worse than *scim*, with its banishment from the latest dictionaries. All the nuanced meanings that surrounded it have gone too. The first part of the word, *lorg*, can at a stretch mean a leg but it more often refers to a footmark, a track, a log, a peg, a staff, a band of followers, progeny, hankering after, desire for or searching for. The word *beart* usually means a parcel, a large woman or a bundle of rushes or straw carried on the back or shoulders. But it can also mean a deed, task, prank or move in a game. So the compound *loirg-bheart* can have myriad meanings that are now all gone.

The word that best expresses the sense of absence or vacuum left by such losses is *iarm-haireacht*, the loneliness you feel at cockcrow, when you are the only person awake and experience that existential pang of disconnection, of not belonging.

I had never quite noticed that tinge of sadness I felt as a child when awake before anyone else – a mix of elation at the tranquil beauty of the scene and regret at having no one to share it with – until my grandmother taught me *iarmhaireacht* one morning when I was seven. She caught me unwrapping a sickle shortly after dawn to go out and hack the grass back from oaks I had planted.

I was aware of the word *díláthair*, which meant absence – but not the absence felt by an early riser or distant lover or anything of that kind. Instead, *díláthair* referred to the absence felt when something or somewhere has been depopulated or destroyed by other human beings. It is the feeling the next generation will experience in a world without coral reefs or glaciers. It's also the feeling our descendants may have when they realise that we willingly chose not to pass this language on to them.

ISLAND SANCTUARY

Handing on the language to her grandchildren was a key motivation for my grandmother Sighle Humphreys in later life. It was she who taught me *forcamás*, the unsteadiness of a stone about to fall, and *bladhmann*, the steam rising from a fermented haystack – which can also refer to the insubstantial boasts of a braggart. She'd take me through how the word *breacadh* can mean the picking of a millstone, the act of explaining something, covering a paper with writing, or the dawn of a new day.

Some people teach their offspring sports, life skills, ideals or business prowess, but for Sighle language represented something beyond all these. She had seen how an immersion in Ireland's traditional language and customs had been the basis for her uncle's act of heroic self-sacrifice (or rash folly, depending on one's viewpoint).

The O'Rahilly's willingness to sacrifice everything to free his compatriots from enslavement to England arose from his mounting realisation of the truth of the statement made by a leading rebel of the preceding generation, Thomas Davis, who wrote that

a people without a language of its own is only half a nation. A nation should guard its language more than its territories – 'tis a surer barrier, and more important frontier, than fortress or rivers.

In her early teens Sighle took on that belief and it was copper-fastened on that Monday morning of Easter Week in 1916. Ever since that moment, she devoted her life to fulfilling The O'Rahilly's vision of an independent, Irish-speaking nation.

This first took the form of fighting England: stealing bullets, hiding guns, carrying secret despatches for rebel leaders, tending to them when they were injured in guerrilla skirmishes and training other women to join the fight. In time Sighle became the vice president of Cumann na mBan, the women's auxiliary army that supported the Irish Republican Army in every way it could.

This became the focus of her life for the next twenty years until her mother and her aunt (The O'Rahilly's sisters) convinced her to give up fighting and find a man to have a family with or risk being disinherited by them. She capitulated, principally because the money she would inherit could be used to further the cause. By that time she had spent three years in prison at different times and endured 31 days on hunger strike, with countless more rough nights spent on the run, hiding from her enemies.

The next phase of Sighle's life would have to be more sedate for the sake of her only surviving child, my mother, but she redoubled her efforts towards promoting the Irish language. My mother's first language was Irish, and Sighle ensured that it would also be ours when we came along thirty years later.

Despite our living in Dublin she made sure that we didn't get to experience any English until we were four or five. Our minders and babysitters were Irish-speakers, our first books and games were in Irish, and television was strictly limited. Once we were old enough to encounter the wider world, she bribed us with sweets and money to learn new Irish words and phrases, and she would read us passages of local Co. Kerry folklore and memoirs, mixed with accounts of Republican propaganda – if, and only if, the Irish in them was suitably eloquent.

My favourite thing was when she'd share stories of her childhood holidays with The O'Rahilly and their extended family on the Dingle Peninsula from 1912 onwards. For the first few years they would go out to stay on the Great Blasket Island, on the very tip of west Co. Kerry. The entire family (Sighle and her mother, brothers and aunt, alongside The O'Rahilly, his wife and four children) would move into the tiny thatched cottage of Cáit Ní Ghuithín, the daughter of the King of the Island (an elected community leader that was common in the social structure of some of the islands off the west coast), or other neighbouring houses, depending on who had a spare patch of floor space.

Through these stories I got to know everyone on the island, including the last king, Pádraig Ó Catháin; the great *seanchaí* (custodian of tradition and storyteller) Peig Sayers; and the author of the classic memoir *An tOileánach* ('The Islandman'), Tomás Ó Criomhthain.

I knew who on the island was a right *manglam*, a thickset boorish person, and who had the sweetest *manglam dod*, a morning croon while preparing breakfast, and who could carry the largest *manglam bog*, an untidy armful of hay. I knew who was best at *margaíocht*, or bargaining, with passing sailors, and who was most adept at *reacaireacht*, which describes bargaining accompanied by impassioned exclamations and non-verbal negotiations – something that was necessary when dealing with the German, English and Russian mariners who occasionally hauled up during the First World War. At its most expansive *reacaireacht* can imply that the goods are worth far more than the price being offered and that, in fact, the seller is making a sacrifice by offering them at this knock-down rate. (I often felt there was a degree of *reacaireacht* to my great-granduncle's martyrdom.)

On the Great Blasket, Sighle experienced a life that was unchanged for centuries: scaling cliffs to gather the eggs of nesting marine birds, butchering seals for lamp oil, grabbing puffins from the air, salvaging flotsam from sunken vessels – all the while being immersed in one of the purest sources of Irish that still existed. It was a form of the language that retained traces of its roots in the Indus Valley in central Asia; you could hear echoes in their dialect of words and phrases that had veered off from Sanskrit, Persian and Hebrew millennia before.

I never got to experience this Blasket Irish in its full glory, as the island was forcibly evacuated by the government in 1953, before I was born, but my brother, Ruán, and I would later spend our summers calling in to the tiny cottages and simple farmhouses of these now elderly former islanders who had been resettled on the mainland.

Why we felt compelled to go visiting the elderly in this way I'm not quite sure, except that, between the ages of eight and twelve, there was not much else for us to do, and my brother had a sweet tooth that was always in search of satiation. The elderly people, being somewhat lonely or simply hospitable, would invite us in and offer us a slice of *bairín breac* ('speckled loaf') or a chocolate Club Milk and glass of concentrated MiWadi orange (which my brother would barely dilute so as to get the full sugar rush).

The old men weren't so interested in us and, in fact, only those suffering from emphysema or arthritis were ever home; the rest were down at the pier watching the young folk prepare to go to sea and then waiting all day for their return in those flimsy canvas *naomhóga* that had been the lifelines of Blasket Island life. It was always the women who fussed over us, calling me their *buachaillín bán*, their fair-headed (or beloved) boy.

We also visited because that practice was the preeminent activity of Gaeltacht life. Life there, at least as I experienced it, was a continual series of visits to neighbouring houses. The ubiquity of it is clear in the variety of words used for such behaviour. *Bothántaíocht* is the most common word, which according to Dinneen's dictionary of 1927 is 'the practice of frequenting neighbours' houses for the purpose of hearing old stories', as opposed to *scoraíocht*, which he defines as a gossiping visit to a neighbour's house. *Cuartaíocht* was a more solemn visit. Dinneen goes on to differentiate between *ionnsaightheach* – visiting in a way that feels aggressive – and *táirdíol*, the act of visiting from house to house in a circuit. The word *fiosrú* means enquiring but also visiting a house with the aim of extracting information, while *éileamh* means a demand or claim but can also be a visit conducted in a friendly manner. A night visit of an amicable form, which at best stretches to singing and dancing by the fireside, is an *airneál*. They can all be summed up as a *tamhach táisc*, which means the sound of voices raised in fun or revelry when people are gathered together. Finally, the word for a visit that outstays its welcome or is overly protracted is *strambán*.

All this is to say that, indirectly, I managed to get a good sense of Blasket Island Irish. I learnt then that *cuillith* is the inner sheaf of a corn stack and could also be the little ripples bounding the current in the middle of a swollen stream. *Stabh* is a burly person and also an iron vessel chained to the side of a well for drinking. *Snáth sracaireachta* is thread used for tying on a bait of crab while fishing for rock fish – although whether these were specifically Blasket words or terms sourced elsewhere by my grandmother I can't be sure.

On one occasion Cáit Ní Chatháin, whose father was a prominent islander and who herself spent a lifetime as a baker's assistant in Springfield, Massachusetts, before retiring to Baile na nGall, just up the road from our house, took me aside to tell me that I had *mianach na farraige ionam*, meaning that the essence of the sea was within me. I never fully understood what she meant by this, but the power and the mystery of it seared into me. It contorted my reality just a little. It was a heady infusion for a young Dublin boy with a Lego and *Star Wars* fixation. I began, over time, to hanker for the past rather than strive for the modern Ireland that Sighle and The O'Rahilly had fought so valiantly for. It was the distorting effect of these things over decades that bound me tightly to the old words and ways that we are now so easily shedding.

DANCING WORDS

The concept of a sound having a direct and lasting impact on the world around us was brought home to me by the word *taoscán*, also the name of a cliff in Valentia Island, Co. Kerry, where the sea mounts up to a considerable height. The moaning of the waves was considered a sign, and even the instigator, of an approaching storm. Thus, the sheer impact of the noise would summon the tempest, just as a shout can call forth an avalanche.

This notion shifted my understanding of the effect that sounds – and more specifically words – can have on the world. This happened around about the time I was getting into baking sweet biscuits at the weekends in my early teens in Dublin, partly inspired by tales Cáit Ní Chatháin had told me of the enormous, chewy chocolate-chip cookies and peanut-butter thins she'd bake in America. These were unknown concepts in Ireland – even the word 'cookie' was heard only in American films and on 'Sesame Street'.

On one occasion when I happened to let flour fall onto the speakers of the kitchen radio, I noticed the tiny white specks begin to dance. The flour particles were jumping into the air in what at first appeared to be random, chaotic leaping; but when the radio presenter on Raidió na Gaeltachta began reciting the words of an old poem, 'An Cailleach Bhéarra', the flour started to arrange itself into more complex patterns.

Initially I felt certain that I was imagining the whole thing and was about to dismiss it, but then

I unscrewed the radio's casing and sprinkled a thin *scim* of flour directly onto the black paper drums of both speakers and watched, transfixed, as the specks of white began to organise themselves into waves, matrices and concentric circles. (You'll recall that *scim* means a thin layer of flour or dust, a fairy film that covers the land, and a succumbing to the supernatural world through sleep.) The specks looked like tiny models of swirling nebulae or vastly magnified cellular organisms.

It was as if the words had come to life – had found a way of manifesting themselves physically. They were dancing in this endlessly adaptive and evolving flux state. I saw imploding stars and the schematics of crystalline molecules – an ever-changing kaleidoscope but with a seemingly regular pattern that could potentially be decoded.

In dancing style it was closer to *damhsa* than *rince*. Both these words mean dancing, but in some dialects *damhsa* is more often used to describe human dancing, while *rince* more often refers to animals. (Pádhraic S. Ó Murchú of Turas Siar

Cultural Centre defines *rince* as what 'the young calf would be doing when it was first let out of the shed. The sunlight would fascinate them, dazzle them. They'd never seen each other or their own shadows before and so they'd start *ag rince*, dancing around.') The flour grains seemed to display elements of both *rince* and *damhsa* but were more aligned to animalistic gyrations; in fact they were closest of all to *macnas*, which means both wantonness and the giddy, frolicsome dancing of young calves when first released into the fields in spring.

The transformation of sound into complex flour shapes was even more arresting as the words happened to be particularly potent. 'An Cailleach Bhéarra' is a powerful lament from many centuries ago and the presenter was reading it in an incantatory manner. (That a radio station would broadcast such material in the middle of the day may seem strange to some, but it's standard for Raidió na Gaeltachta, the national Irish-language station, which regularly explores folklore and customs between playing traditional airs and discussing fishing quotas and reporting local death notices. I would often hear Cáit Ní Chatháin on the radio, retelling old stories from the mythological tradition or recounting events that happened to her father on the Blaskets long ago.)

Recently I heard an afternoon phone-in discussion on Raidió na Gaeltachta in which the terms used to describe lust in animals were discussed. The three contributors, each from a different Gaeltacht area and representing markedly different dialects, argued over the precise meaning and pronunciation of almost all the words. Those they mostly agreed on were *dáir*, the desire for copulation among cattle; *clíth*, the same desire among swine; *eachmhairt* for horses; *snafach* for donkeys; *reith* for sheep; *imreas* for goats; *soidhir* for dogs; *bocachas* for rabbits; *láth* for deer; and *catachas* for cats. For any other animal you could probably get away with *rachmall*, *drúis*, *adhall* or *ratamas*, depending on which Gaeltacht you were in and what dialect you spoke. The above-mentioned *macnas* can also refer to being overcome by the lusts of the flesh.

But back to the flour particles. That the word for a tiny speck of flour, *cáithnín*, is also the word for the tiniest specks of physical life, or a subatomic particle, seemed significant, especially considering that a further meaning of *cáithnín* is the goose-bumps you feel when, for example, you ponder the interrelatedness of things and how small we are in relation to the whole. Given this, I like the fact that *cáithnín* can also mean an atom, a husk of corn, a snowflake, a minuscule smidge of butter or anything tiny that gets into the eye and irritates it.

I simply couldn't work out how these particles would suddenly take on a life of their own in this way and how they were responding in such a tangible way to the sound of the words. I became determined to find out and kept asking everyone I met until, finally, my godmother told me about nodal patterns and how they would make parts of the speaker membrane vibrate in opposite directions when resonating. She went on to tell me that, when people speak, the sounds sent from our vocal folds pulsate outwards, colliding with the surrounding air and generating longitudinal pressure waves within the air. This would account for what I saw on the speakers, but the complexity of the patterns and their specificity to each word seemed to imply more.

I wondered whether these nodal patterns stretched across the membrane of the world and if so whether the words we utter have tiny vibrational effects on the physical matter surrounding us, or at least their underlying energetic properties. It also brought home to me the profound impact that every word I speak might be having on the world, even if I was oblivious of it.

Recently I played a recording I made of myself speaking Irish and then English and Spanish through larger flour-sprinkled speakers, and the patterns were markedly different, with seemingly less malleability in the patterns made by the other languages, although it is hard to be objective about such things, and I was naturally biased towards the Irish sounds.

That different languages 'dance' differently in the world is not so far-fetched: we know that sound is a vibration that travels through a medium, whether gas, liquid or solid. If you strike a bell, for example, the bell vibrates in the air; as one side of it moves out it pushes the air molecules next to it, increasing the pressure in that region of space. This area of higher pressure becomes a compression. As the side of the bell moves back in, it pulls the molecules apart, creating a lower-pressure region called a 'rarefaction'. Each one of these back-and-forths is a wavelength, which becomes part of a sound wave.

The number of wave cycles that occur in one second is measured as frequency, and just as each bell has its own frequency, so too does each language. Chinese is higher in frequency than English, and Irish is generally lower than English, depending on the dialect and the speaker. Hungarian is even lower again. Thus, the air particles in the room will vibrate at a lower pitch with an Irish word than with an English one. The difference is only about half an octave between Chinese and Hungarian, but it's noticeable to the human ear. It's one way we can discern whether someone is a native speaker or not.

One stormy Christmas I spent a weekend in an old lighthouse worker's cottage in Co. Donegal and watched as the air pressure from the Atlantic waves pummelling the seawall sent the tea in my cup spilling over. By singing a soothing lullaby to the tea I was able to calm it again, easing the surface tension, perhaps. I got my friend to try singing to her cup and the effect was different. Not only does each language have its own frequency but so too do individual speakers. The sound waves of our words have a frequency related to the frequency patterns of our vocal folds – so my speaking Irish will have a different effect from the same words spoken by someone raised entirely in that frequency.

There's no doubt that sound affects reality; it's just that we have a choice about whether to be conscious of it or not. Yet the idea that particular Irish phrases, when said aloud, can affect an environment still sounds like a step too far. Maybe it's just so basic that we've overlooked it or have never stopped to analyse it.

For, why else do we start talking to ourselves to banish darkness or sing to ourselves when drenched with rain? It's partly a psychological crutch to ease our inner selves but at some level we also feel that the world is transformed and becomes safer, warmer and more knowable when our language is emanating through it. This is why, I think, I like speaking my native tongue. It makes the world around me feel more familiar.

Animals respond differently to Irish too, in my experience, though I'm not claiming this as fact. They clearly don't understand the words but there appears to be something in the sounds, as I can get any angry dog to turn back home by shouting the phrase *buail abhaile*, 'head off home'. This phrase has worked for me not just in Ireland but all over South America and Africa. Dogs invariably turn around and skulk back to where they belong. (I even once tried it on a black bear in British Columbia, but at the last minute I lost my nerve and sprayed pepper spray, which may have had more of an effect.)

Yet farmers will argue that there are many words that have a direct and visible impact on animals. In West Kerry *ceartaigh*, meaning 'to amend or compose yourself', will get a cow to stand in the correct position for milking, while in Connemara they respond better to *deasaigh*, 'settle yourself in position'. *Dráinín*, meaning 'little grinner or snarler', can be used in various Gaeltacht areas with different dialects to calm a cow while milking her.

There are other onomatopoeic words, such as *beada, beada*, which will bring geese to their food, and *finic*, which will call ducks home from their wandering – but, again, this works best in Co. Clare. In Co. Monaghan the ducks respond better to *fit*.

If you want to keep hens away from something, you say *scearc*, while to call them in for food or for protection from the fox you say *diuc*, meaning 'confound you'. It also implies a stooping of the shoulders. In Cos. Monaghan and Cavan there are references to *diuc* being pronounced with more stress on the 'u' so that the word becomes *diúc*. In Co. Westmeath hens responded best to *tiuc*.

There'd be no point saying *diuc, diúc* or *tiuc* to a pig; for them *bach* is the word that will call them to their slops, according to Diarmuid Ó Muirithe's *Dictionary of Anglo-Irish*. The word *bach* also means a rout and a display of angry drunkenness.

The effect of these words on the world should not be underestimated. For example, *dorr* has a dramatically opposite effect to *buail abhaile* and should be used only with caution, if at all. It can incite dogs to war, and in some counties it will provoke a wicked ram, prone to butting, to start misbehaving. Elsewhere the word is used to further annoy an angry bull, and so, to be safe, it's best to avoid it entirely.

THE WAVE

The word *taoscán* refers not only to a cliff with a particular moaning wave on Valentia Island but also to a glass of spirits or to the quantity of any liquid poured into a vessel. It suggests a generous amount of liquid, as in the state of being reasonably full or more than half full, or of flowing bountifully. There's an optimistic sense of plenty to it, without suggesting excess. I've heard it used to describe any fairly large quantity of liquid, such as milk or beer, but also of butter, lime, hay or other material that is not entirely solid. A core element is that it always implies that there is room for more. It suggests enough or even plenty but never too much. Its root meaning is 'pouring' or 'flowing'.

The malleability of meaning encompassed by *taoscán* suggests again the Irish language's similarity to waves in the sea more than to a specific linguistic code of communication. The word *cuilithe* describes the way chat and gossip can run through a community while also being used for the small ripples running through the middle of a swollen stream or river, or for an eddying current at sea. Likewise, the phrase *tarraing anuas* means both the introduction of a topic of conversation and a groundswell or waves dashing against rocks. *Tulca* can mean both speaking fluently and a large sea wave. It also means a horn-led charge.

The thing about waves is that they are unique, each one different from the next, and yet all are connected as a whole, working on a far greater scale than we can readily imagine. The tsunami in the Indian Ocean in 2004 sent water rising in wells around Ireland, as was recorded at a hydrographic monitoring station in Kilkenny and reported on by Peadar McArdle, former director of the Irish Geological Survey. The tsunami was caused by something else entirely, separate and far away, off the west coast of Sumatra, where tectonic plates that had been grinding for thousands of years suddenly cracked, causing trillions of tons of rock to move with the power of 23,000 Hiroshima-type atomic bombs. Everything is separate, yet everything is connected.

Irish recognises this dichotomy in its principal word for wave, *tonn*, which can mean both a single wave and the entire ocean, depending on the context. *Thar toinn* means abroad, though it literally translates as 'over the waves', while *faoi thoinn* means 'submarine' or 'under the waves'. The word *tonn* also refers to the skin or surface of something, or low-lying land, or a level marsh, or the hide of an animal, or something nimble. As a verb it can mean to pour, gush or surge. *Fear tuinne* is used as a fond term for salmon, though it translates literally as 'man of the waves'.

The motion of waves rising through the ocean is known as *tonnadh*, which can also mean vomiting, belching or convulsing, and it's a word used to describe death by poison. It is not to be confused with *tonnach*, which means wavy and tempestuous, or with *tonach*, which is the act of preparing a corpse for waking, that is, washing the body and sewing the mouth closed. As a verb *tonaim* means 'I close the mouth of a dead person and prepare them for death.' The word can also be used to suggest throwing in the towel, as in *táim go hiomlán tonach*, 'I'm totally spent.'

The preeminent waves in Irish mythology all have names and they are both sea and sound waves. The best known are Tonn Tuaithe, Tonn Rudhraighe and Tonn Clíodhna. These are super-natural forces that thunder around the island's perimeter, protecting the land, binding and controlling existence, much like particle or grav-itational forces. It was one of these waves that conspired to lift the ships of Amergin and his people safely to shore when humans first settled here. But, long before that, when the god of skill and art, Lugh, first left the magical realm of Tír na nÓg ('Land of Youth') to come to Ireland it is said that 'the little crystal waves lifted themselves up to look at him' and then followed him here, where 'the Three Great Waves of Ireland thundered a welcome'. It is often the noise of waves, rather than their tidal quality, that is most apparent to us, emphasising the fact that they are just as much auditory as aqueous.

Potentially they are older even than Lugh. Geographers claim that Tonn Rudhraighe (the Wave of Rudraige), which can still be seen and heard in Dundrum Bay, Co. Down, may have originated in a folk memory of the glacial flood that poured out of southern Lough Neagh through Poyntzpass, Co. Armagh, and into Carlingford Lough after the Ice Age, when the first settlers were streaming in.

Tonn Tuaithe could also be a memory of the great torrents of gushing water that swept off the land down the Northern Bann River from the north of Lough Neagh for decades and even centuries as the Scottish ice sheet was gradually withdrawing northwards towards the Arctic. This wave appears to be the same one that picked up chalk debris from Ireland's northern coast and swept it out to Rathlin Island to form a gravel bank in the Church Bay area over ten thousand years ago.

Just think about this for a moment. It's a mind-spinning concept and goes a long way towards explaining why Ireland has such a different feel from the rest of Europe. Many inhabitants are descendants of the original settlers who arrived in one of the numerous waves of migration since the Ice Age. We've been working the same land and speaking the same language for thousands of years. The continuity of tradition and lore is more like the Aboriginals in Australia than anything you'll find elsewhere in Europe.

It is possible that we have somehow managed to cling on to a memory of the gushing waters of the glaciers that our predecessors encountered when they first arrived here. We've embedded this memory in our earliest myths and legends, in which floods and waves of destruction are a constant motif, and we've infused it into our language. Of course, some of the references are post-Christian allusions to the Biblical flood, but Christianity arrived here only in the fifth century, and many of these words and tales are far older than that. It is no wonder that people sense something different here. We are rooted to the island and the natural cycles that caused it, stretching back to the time of glaciers and ice sheets.

WAVE AS GODDESS

Of the three great waves, Tonn Clíodhna ('Clíodhna's wave') is the best known, and it can still be heard on rare occasions rising up out of the cliff caves beyond Glandore Harbour in West Cork. It is named after a goddess who cared for three magic birds with voices so sweet that they could cure all illness. Clíodhna was drowned while hiding in the form of a wren to escape her progenitor, the principal sea god Manannán, who wanted to do one of three things, depending on which version you hear: take back her power, limit her freedom or crush the love she had for a young human, Ciabhán of the Curling Locks. The wave that killed her now lives on as an eerie thunderous roar that bellows out from the cliff rocks in certain weather. It's as much a sound wave as a sea wave now – a loud and sudden call that, for some families, foretells the death of someone significant.

I've met people in Co. Down who claim to have heard Tonn Rudhraighe rising up across the land from Dundrum Bay, though I've never heard it myself. That you can still hear a *tonn* that was sent out from the Otherworld thousands of years ago is stirring. I managed to record what I thought was Tonn Clíodhna once when I happened to be in West Cork during foul weather. When I played it back into the floured speakers, the patterns took on an even greater level of elaboration. It was as if the audio had captured the multifaceted aspects of the wave – that it had been infused with the essence of a fairy goddess after it had killed her, and was now a scion, or the progeny, of the sea god Manannán and so was infused with his quintessential self too.

Of course, younger Irish-speakers and learners don't necessarily think of Tonn Clíodhna when they say the word *tonn*. Yet the word is still imbued with those layers of tradition for older folk – with the birds that cure all illnesses and with Manannán's desire to create a beautiful wave-woman and with his later rash impulse to destroy her. The awareness of all this is still just about clinging on to the word, though how long it will remain so is uncertain.

Yet another layer on top of the audible and liquid waves is the emotional one. For, as well as being sound and sea waves, Tonn Clíodhna and her sibling waves, Tonn Tuaithe and Tonn Rudhraighe, are also waves of emotion that act in sympathy with certain magical beings. Tonn Clíodhna is infused with the sadness of the unfortunate bird-loving fairy goddess that Manannán condemned to death. The wave therefore now has the emotional burden of being a harbinger of death for certain old clans, such as the McCarthys and Collinses. Anyone who has heard Clíodhna wailing up from the rocks during a storm will attest to her forlornness. Thus, these waves are as much psychological entities as anything. We hear their empathetic roar again in the saga of Deirdre and the Sons of Uisneach. When the beautiful Deirdre elopes to Scotland with her lover, Naoise, so as to avoid having to marry the elderly King Conchubor, they find themselves lured back to fight, and in the ensuing vicious battle Conchubor's son Fiacha is forced to crouch behind the shelter of his magical shield – *a bhfoghar gotha graineamhuil le mhead an éigin araibh Fiacha* ('which roared with a horrible vocal sound because of the greatness of Fiacha's distress').

At this moment of anguish and pain the three chief Waves of Ireland roared out in sympathy with the shield. Their wave of distress in turn radiated and was felt by Conall Cernach, a son of Amergin (our original druidic founder), and Conall Cernach races up to Armagh and plunges into the melee, accidentally killing Illann, the son of Naoise's protector, then beheads himself out of guilt.

Not only are the waves now capable of communicating but so too is this shield, which was called Ochain. The Táin Bó Cuailnge saga claimed that Ochain could make the shields of all Ulstermen groan in an emotional resonance. The name of this shield possibly derives from *Och*, as in the exclamation 'Ah!', to which was added *caíne* (*caoineadh*, meaning 'keening' or 'weeping'). But it is also often called Aicein, from the Old Irish word for ocean. This would account for its sympathy with the three waves that were occasionally regarded as the wave-daughters of the sea god Manannán (the same one whom Tuatha Dé Danann told to churn up the seas when Amergin and our ancestors were trying to land).

Thus, the waves are oceanic, vocal and emotional ... as is the shield. They are all known to prophesy the deaths of others, and they can protect people and become aqueous in certain circumstances. That's quite an expanse of references to keep in mind when using the word *tonn* in general conversation, but it's actually typical of the multidimensional matrices that are connected to certain words in old languages.

I could delve deeper into the similarities and interrelatedness of waves and shields in Irish, but the principal notion here is that almost any two elements of Irish have intrinsic connections. That is just the way of things with ancient cultures. They form an ecosystem that is as interconnected and nuanced as any biosphere – or as a sacred bell, cast from an amalgam or alloy of tin, zinc, iron, lead and sweet-sounding copper.

BLARNEY

The Blarney Stone in Co. Cork that reputedly gives those who kiss it the gift of eloquence might seem like another touristic gimmick, such as leprechaun hats, Irish coffee and turning rivers green on St Patrick's Day; but some say that it too is based on Clíodhna and her wave.

The 400,000 tourists a year who pay €16 to kiss a seemingly random lump of carboniferous limestone appear to be being hoodwinked, but while queuing to ascend Blarney Castle's treacherous stone stairway recently, I met a man who changed my view. As we were winding our way up to the battlements, where the enchanted stone is built into the crenellations, he told me that it was Clíodhna who had bestowed on it its ability to foster loquaciousness. I didn't believe him at first, but within seconds he had called up academic sources on his phone that laid out her connection to the site. It suddenly seemed apt that this fairy being who had once been a torrent of glacial water pouring off the land after the Ice Age would now release torrents of *béarla* ('speech') in others.

Most people are now familiar with the word *Béarla* only with a capital 'B', meaning 'English', but the word originally meant 'language' or 'speech'. Thus, there was *Gaeilge* ('Irish', a language believed to have been given to the world as the only perfect language after the fall of the Tower of Babel, which was caused by the unintelligibility arising from too many languages), and *béarla*, which was random, inarticulate speech. As Irish people became aware of other languages, they gave them each a unique name in the feminine gender, but English was never granted that distinction and is still referred to only as *Béarla*, which is a masculine word.

The Blarney Castle man went on to tell me that Clíodhna was not dead and that still today she exerts an influence on certain families in the region. I raised a wary eyebrow, but he was insistent.

'How could she die?' he asked, 'when she was a goddess from the Otherworld. The wave sent by Manannán only drowned a certain aspect of her. It didn't kill her outright.'

He went on to tell me that he knew people who still referred to Tonn Clíodhna as a metaphor for a terrible storm, and since then I've heard the phrase myself used to convey a forlorn feeling or a tragedy. That is only in Irish, however: its other layers of meaning haven't transferred to the English form, Clíodhna's Wave.

Some of the distinguished Munster families for whom she has played a crucial role for the past few hundred years still claim an allegiance to her. The principal family that she was allied with was the Uí

Fidgheinte sept, who later became the O'Donovan and O'Collins families. They ruled the land she frequented between the fourth and tenth centuries, and when this territory was taken over by the MacCarthys and Fitzgeralds she switched allegiance to them and became their *bean sí* ('banshee', 'fairy woman'). She would advise them telepathically on important issues or send messengers to warn them of imminent danger, or even on occasion appear in person to them in times of great need.

It is said that in the 15th century the King of Desmond, Cormac MacCarthy, owner of Blarney Castle, consulted her on a complicated legal matter and she advised him that, to possess the eloquence and focus needed in the court in London, he must kiss the first stone he saw on the morning he left Ireland for the trial. So beneficial did her advice prove that he won the case and immediately moved the stone to its current remote site on the parapet so that others could not access it. This hasn't quite worked out as intended, given the hundreds of thousands of visitors who now seek it out as a priority on arriving in Ireland, but at least it helps keep Clíodhna's memory alive.

In the 16th century, Clíodhna was still active in our world, with reports that she had an affair with Earl Gerald Fitzgerald of the eminent Gaelic sept the Desmond Geraldines, who lived in Glin Castle, Co. Limerick. And even up to the 19th century there are references to her existence in a republication of a medieval genealogy that refers to a son of the O'Leary family from Co. Cork being Conor Clíodhna – a child of the fairy goddess herself. Then, in the 20th century, a leading Irish revolutionary and chairman of the Provisional Government, Michael Collins, acknowledged his kinship with her through his family lineage of the O'Collinses of Carbery in Co. Cork.

Michael Collins spent his youth playing around Clíodhna's Rock, an unassuming outcrop of grey boulders in the parish of Kilshannig, near Mallow, which Clíodhna is said to have haunted. Among the rocks is an opening that was said to be the entrance to her palace within the hill, and from there she ruled as Queen of the Fairies of South Munster.

There are reports of regular gatherings of all the fairies of Ireland at this spot, and in 1906 Colonel James Grove White wrote: 'Even under the midday sun one would feel solitary and uneasy while there alone, as if the enchantress had infused her mystical and dark art into every part of it.' A generation ago people were still claiming to have seen Clíodhna, dressed in otherworldly gowns and leading the May Eve dance of her followers by the light of the moon.

I visited the rock a few summers ago and, with a mix of embarrassment and apprehension, tried to make contact with Clíodhna, using the method practised by a local folk healer, Caitlín Óg Chéitinn, long ago. Caitlín had gone to the rock to confront the dead goddess after a local poet, Séamas Mac Gearailt, died shortly after his engagement to a woman. It was believed that he had been kidnapped by Clíodhna, so Caitlín stood at the rock entrance and demanded that she return him, using a form of poetic verse believed to arouse members of the

Otherworld. Clíodhna didn't appear but uttered a defence of herself from within the rock using the same complex metrical form and making it clear that she wouldn't return the man under any circumstances.

On the day I approached her rock I didn't intend to accuse her of anything: I just wanted to find out how things were going for her. I stood there in the middle of the field and began chanting while some shorthorn cattle glanced suspiciously at me. It was hard to concentrate on the accuracy of my metrical pronunciations, as I was anxious that the farmer might appear at any moment, but in the end I had no success in raising Clíodhna. Perhaps my metrical skills weren't up to scratch.

FAIRY WORDS

The whole notion of Clíodhna and her magical wave siblings leads us into the realm of fairies. It is hard to proceed far into considering Irish without coming to some understanding of this topic. Many Irish words are so imbued with elements of the Otherworld that a speaker really ought to clarify their own relationship with the spirit beings before attempting to learn the language. Though the idea is derided or denied now, for eons our people believed that fairies lived beneath the earth, and for some people they are still a presence in their lives. Even if you no longer accept the existence of fairies, you cannot help but encounter them in many words and place names.

The word for 'kidnap', for example, is *fuadach*, and you'll hear it regularly on the news to refer to criminal abductions, but that's not what it used to mean. *Fuadach* meant being spirited away or carried off by the fairies. That was how earlier dictionaries defined it, but newer publications have conveniently forgotten this.

There was a word to describe the empty husk or changeling that was left behind when the fairies whisked away a person's spirit or soul – typically it was a defenceless child or an unattached woman who was targeted. This word was *iarmhar*, but now that meaning has itself been kidnapped and replaced with something else. *Iarmhar* has come to mean a remnant or spent residue of something, such as the dregs in a bottle of wine or the crumbs in a toaster.

Other words are code for fairies, because the actual word, *Sí* or *sióga*, should never be uttered in their presence ... and you should always assume that they are present. It's best to refer to them as *Na Daoine Maithe* ('the Good People') or *na hUaisle* ('the Gentry'). Therefore, *áit uasal* can mean either a noble place or a fairy region, depending on the context.

Among the innumerable other words for the supernatural folk who live beneath the earth are *bunadh na gcnoc* ('the folk of the hill'), *muintir an leasa* ('the crowd fostering your wellbeing'), *na daoine beaga* ('the little people') and *scaoth*, which means a swarm or multitude of mostly flying things such as birds and bees but also refers to fairies. *Aeróg* means an antenna but also an aerial being, such as a fairy. *Fíothal* means scrubland or a fairy of the goblin variety. *Diúch* is a windpipe or gullet but also an elf.

Even the common verb *teastaigh*, to want or need (or to feel the absence of), has the additional meaning of being wanted by the fairies. The phrase *Theastaigh an bhean sin* therefore means either 'that woman wanted' or 'she was wanted by the fairies and therefore taken by them'.

The primary meaning of *trioplóg* is a tuft of grass or a small cluster of something natural, but in some contexts it can mean a fairy spell. The word *geasróg* generally refers to a spell as well, but it differs from the others in that it can be used for a charm cast by either a fairy or a human. As with the other terms it also has a modern, rational connotation when used to refer to superstition.

Perhaps the form of fairy that has caused the most controversy is the leprechaun. It's a sensitive issue for Irish people, because of the way it was handled in 19th-century English and American journals and most particularly in the Disney film *Darby O'Gill and the Little People* (1959). Its depiction of leprechauns came to be used to mock Irish people and was later commodified to help sell legions of tacky souvenirs.

But Walt Disney in fact based the depiction of leprechauns on reports compiled by the Irish Government documenting people's attitude to the spirit folk. It was a national research project called the Schools Manuscripts Collection that ran for 18 months from 1937 and produced more than half a million pages of material that was gathered by 100,000 children from their grandparents, grand-uncles and grand-aunts, as well as from older members of the community. The collection contains more than 375 accounts of leprechauns, from practically every county, ranging from 39 in rural Co. Cork to a single one in Co. Louth. It can therefore hardly be considered culturally insensitive to refer to leprechauns or to our past belief in them.

To take two examples, there's an account in the collection by Patrick Donoghue, a farmer from Raharney, Co. Westmeath, who was 85 in 1937.

> At a bridge called the 'wild cats bridge' about two miles from the village of Raharney a leprecaun is seen playing a bagpipes at the bridge every night at twelve o clock. At the other side of the road it is said that there is a pot of gold buried and a turkey hen left to mind it.

For Donoghue, this was just a piece of local knowledge. It was a fact, just as how we are now told to believe that the molecules in a table are constantly moving, even though most of us will never see this with our own eyes. Donoghue went on to say that John Kellet of Raharney

is supposed to have caught a leipreachan. He asked him to give him the gold. He said he would and then he said to John that his wife was calling to him and when John turned round the leipreachan went away.

His neighbour Pat Farrelly, a former labourer, remembered a time when Tommy Scally

was spreading manure and while he was doing so a leipreachan appeared and walked around the cart looking at it. The man, who had never seen such a thing before, fainted and had to be carried off. A few weeks after he was out in the field again and the leipreachan appeared. The man caught him by the shoulder but he disappeared out of his hands.

These are just two among hundreds of tales of encounters with leprechauns, which still exert a certain influence on the language and are frequently referred to in place names. The word derives from *lúchorpán*, a small body, but the varieties of it make it clear that leprechauns never had a single, easily definable character.

The most common term is *gréasaí leipreachán* (a little-bodied cobbler), but one can also find references to *lutharacán, lorgadán, lúracán, lochradán, lochramán, loimreachán, loiridín, luadhacán, luiricín, lúiridín, lutharadán, lutharagán* and *luacharmán*. Each word was indigenous to an area. *Lutharacán, lorgadán* and *lúracán* are from the Iveragh Peninsula, the Limerick–Tipperary border and the region around Kilkenny and South Wexford, respectively. Other versions have strayed further from the base version, such as *clutharacán*, which is found only in a remote area bordering West Cork and East Kerry; *geacánach* was used from South Ulster down through the stretch of Leinster north of the River Boyne. On the Aran island of Inis Meáin the word *lioprachán* is used, while just across the water in Cois Fharraige and Carna the same word means a baby bird.

The leprechauns in each area shared the characteristic of being small, and almost all carried with them an inexhaustible fairy purse, which could be yours if you could catch hold of one of the creatures. They were like the lottery, always offering the outside chance of unimaginable wealth.

Other leprechauns, with slightly different traits, had other names. In the Hiberno-English of Co. Fermanagh a gankeenock (from *geancáneach*, 'fairy cobbler') was a typical leprechaun, while a lockreeman (from *lochramán*, 'puny creature') was bigger than a fairy but smaller than a typical person. West Limerick had *lutharagáns*, *clutharacáns* and *lorgadáns*. The first of these referred to a run-of-mill leprechaun, while the second and third were used for smaller and heavier-set ones, respectively. The Blasket Island poet Mícheál Ó Gaoithín, son of Peig Sayers, referred to *loprachán*, *lochargán*, *lotharagán*, *lopracháinín* and *lochargáinín* all within the span of a single story.

Leprechauns have always been part of my Irish-language life in West Kerry, though in my English-language life in Dublin they were confined to films and storybooks. When I was about seven, while digging in the garden between Muiríoch and Baile na nGall, I found an old *dúidín*, a short-stemmed clay pipe, with its stem broken off. Most pipes like these are from the mid-19th century to the early 20th century, and they can be dated accurately by means of the design stamped on them. Mine was stamped *IRISH TRADES ASSOCIATION*, which dates it to about 1870, but when I showed it to an elderly neighbour, Maidhc Idá, he insisted it was a *pipín lutharagáin*, a leprechaun's pipe. He said it with such conviction – and the pipe looked so ancient and otherworldly – that I had no cause to doubt him. It was he who told me that the pig nuts I had dug up beneath ash trees were *prátaí lutharagáin* ('leprechaun potatoes') and he had said it in such a way that I never thought to question it. I accepted it as a fact, just as he did, for after all we weren't far from the *lios* ('fairy fort') where my mother is sure she saw a leprechaun when she was a girl. She was an only child with a vivid imagination and no cousins or friends nearby to play with, so I can readily believe her.

TABOO

The principal reason for the matter of fairies being so complex in Irish is that there was a *geis* on using the word for them, which is *síoga*. But to understand this idea we first need to unpack what a *geis* is, which can, if necessary, be translated as 'taboo', although that doesn't convey all, or even much, of its true meaning. In some circumstances *geis* can refer to a spell but that is mostly the type of spell that places a binding injunction on someone.

A *geis* was often a means by which women controlled men in ways that didn't require physical superiority but that instead introduced an element of shaming or of threatening a person's honour. Breaking a *geis* brought disgrace and risked one's standing in society.

But a *geis* can also be a gift; if you know of a certain threat to a person, you can place a *geis* on them not to go to that place or take part in that activity. It could help steer them on the right path without letting them know the risks of taking a different route.

Through this prism, a *geis* becomes more a matter of destiny than of control. Finding yourself in a position in which you might have to break a *geis* is a sign that you've strayed from the righteous path and that the gods aren't happy with you. Or that life isn't going your way and that it's time to reassess your actions.

The consequences of breaking a *geis* were always bad, ranging from dishonour to misfortune and even death. However, observing the strictures of your *geis* can bring power and it shows others that you are aligned with the women in your life, as it is normally they who have set the *geis*.

Cú Chulainn had a *geis* that forbade him to eat the flesh of a hound. He tried hard to honour it but he was eventually tricked into breaking it. He later imposed a *geis* on his unborn son Connla, and many years afterwards Connla's determination to uphold this *geis* led to his death at the hands of the very man who had set it, his father. A well-judged *geis* could really complicate life, as well as add great tension to any tale.

In the story 'Togail Bruidne Da Derga' ('The Destruction of Da Derga's Hostel') the high king Conaire Mór had a range of *geiseanna* imposed on him. They bound every aspect of his life: he wasn't able to sleep in a house that had a fire or any light visible from outside, nor could he leave his fort at Tara every ninth night. He couldn't travel *deiseal* ('sunwise' or 'clockwise') around the Hill of Tara or *tuathal* ('withershins' or 'anticlockwise') around Bregia. He couldn't kill any bird, nor was he allowed to settle quarrels between any two of his subjects. 'Three Reds' were not permitted to go before him into the 'Red's house', nor could there be any plunder committed during his reign.

Given such conditions Conaire was bound to fail, and it was not long before he found himself forced to break one of his *geiseanna* to avoid an even worse fate. This sparked a chain reaction that led him to break each one in turn. Eventually he was compelled to enter the Red House, or hostel, owned by Da Derga 'Red God', after three red-haired horsemen wearing red frocks with red mantles, carrying red spears and riding red steeds, arrived before him.

Once inside, Conaire noticed a lone woman coming to the door seeking to be admitted, and immediately it was clear that he would have to break yet another taboo: an unaccompanied woman could not enter any house he was in after sunset. The lone woman is described, in a translation by Whitley Stokes, as having shins that were as long as a weaver's beam [and] dark as the back of a stag-beetle. A greyish, wooly mantle she wore. Her lower hair used to reach as far as her knee. Her lips were on one side of her head.

Conaire asked her name but was unimpressed with her reply of 'Cailb'. She launched back at him, asserting: 'Many are my names besides.' Then, adopting the pose of magical incantation (standing on one leg and holding up one hand), she began to list her other names.

Samon, Sinand, Seisclend, Sodb, Caill, Coll, Díchóem, Dichiúil, Díthím, Díchuimne, Dichruidne, Dairne, Dáríne, Déruaine, Egem, Agam, Ethamne, Gním, Cluiche, Cethardam, Níth, Némain, Nóennen, Badb, Blosc, Bloár, Huae, óe Aife la Sruth, Mache, Médé, Mod.

From this, Conaire realised that she was a figure from the Otherworld, and he asked her what she wanted.

'That which thou, too, desirest,' she answered,

knowing that by now he was under her spell and that he would do her bidding.

He then made it clear that he was forbidden by his *geis* 'to receive the company of one woman after sunset', but she soon forced him to disregard this restriction, despite his offering to give her an ox and a bacon pig if she agreed to leave.

As if he was not in enough trouble already, Conaire then spotted a man by the fireside with cropped black hair so spiky that if 'a sackful of wild apples were flung on his crown, not an apple would fall on the ground'. He had one eye, one foot and one hand, and he was tending to a bald, black-singed pig that was squealing continually. Conaire recognised him as Fer Caille, 'Man of the Woods', a herdsman whose buttocks were 'the size of a cheese on a withe' and whose wife had a lower lip that reached down to her knee. The couple had earlier tried to entice Conaire on his way to the hostel. The sight of him and his pig together is yet another of Conaire's *geiseanna*. The repercussions of all this are predictably awful.

A person learning Irish today is unlikely to have any conception of the complexity of *geiseanna* and of how they affected many words related to the Otherworld. Thus, the vocabulary such a learner encounters is a diluted version of the real thing. When they use the term *ailse* for 'cancer', they are unlikely to know that it is also a disparaging term for a particularly mischievous form of fairy, since modern dictionaries no longer include it ... but native speakers still know. For them, *braon ailse* could mean both a chemotherapy drip treatment and magical fairy droplets that fall on the tombs of certain tyrants, causing rot.

When a native speaker uses the word *badhbh* for a hooded crow, there is in the word the memory of its earlier homonym, which refers to a female fairy who appears in phantom bird form to certain families. The word also has a third meaning – someone who places curses on others – but these latter meanings haven't made it into modern dictionaries and so will soon be lost.

That a new generation of urban learners is studying Irish is a positive thing, and it's probably best not to mention that they are learning a ghost form of Irish lacking nuance. The word *iarmhar* — the empty husk of someone when the fairies have taken their essence — seems relevant again.

Yet any speaker who attains a degree of fluency will have worked out that the language is built on an acceptance of unknowable realms and dimensions. Even if it is not spelt out in exercise books and learning apps, they'll notice that a word like *brú* is the word for a hostel (or a mansion or fort) but also for an underground fairy palace. The phrase *Tá an Wi-Fi níos fearr sa bhrú* means either that the Wi-Fi is better 'in the hostel' or 'in the fairy fort', depending on context. In the tale 'Togail Bruidne Da Derga', mentioned above, *bruíon* (or *bruiden* in Old Irish) refers to both a hostel and a fairy palace.

To the learner it might seem at first puzzling that *b'é* (a contraction of *ba é*) is the past tense of the verb 'to be' but that its near homonym *bé* is a word for a woman or maiden that can also be used

111

for a fairy or someone with divine powers. They will learn that such exclamations as *Donn, a dhuine!*, which is still heard among older people in Co. Clare, can be translated as 'By God' but that, instead of invoking the Christian God, it calls on Donn, the fairy monarch of Co. Clare who lived in sandbanks near the surf reefs of Lehinch. He was one of Tuatha Dé Danann, a divine race that, it is said, once populated Ireland and that was descended from the god Dagda, who in turn was descended from the ancient Mother Earth figure, Ana, herself thought to be the same god that Hindus worship as Danu or Ama.

The Irish-language learner must also come to realise that there are certain words that, even if used widely, are sometimes unsuitable for use in certain circumstances. For example, while out fishing, one should never mention the Irish word for priest, pig or weasel. These are fine and appropriate on land, but on sea it is taboo to mention them. Instead, one refers to a priest as 'the man with the white collar', to a pig as 'cold irons' and to a weasel as 'the noble little old woman'.

FAIRY PSYCHOLOGY

What is lost if we forget the presence of the Otherworld entities that are encoded within so many words and place names? This underlay of fairy awareness was already seriously diminished by the concerted efforts of the Church, which for centuries worked to remove pagan elements from the language, substituting Christian terms.

In many respects the Church was successful, to the extent that it is now said that you cannot be agnostic and speak Irish. The Irish for 'hello' is *dia duit* (literally 'God be with you'), and 'good luck' is *Beannacht Dé ort* (literally 'the blessing of God on you'). The principal way to express the term 'hopefully' when I was young was *Le cabhair Dé* ('with the help of God'), although the term *táim ag súil* ('I am hoping') is also used. The phrase for 'fortunately' was *buíochas le Dia* ('thanks be to God'), though *go hámharach* is becoming more common.

So, you might think that Christianity has replaced the Otherworld as the esoteric essence that underlies the language, but the use of the word *Dia* (and its genitive *Dé*) does not necessarily imply the Old or New Testament God with the long beard resplendent on a throne. Irish took on the Latin word *Deus*, which the missionaries who arrived in the fifth century were keen to propagate, but many still defined it with their old awareness of an animistic deity. This was a god of all things, of every raindrop and honeysuckle petal – an illuminating life force that infused everything with sanctity.

This old outlook remains, as can be seen in the many pagan practices that continue to animate

Catholicism in Ireland today, from lighting bonfires on St John's Night to weaving rushes for St Brigid's Day. The *Dia* ('God') of Irish is an expansive, supernatural entity rooted in nature, and it is the awareness of this that we risk losing. The psychological benefit of having another dimension of existence living among us cannot be underestimated. The relief it offers is familiar to every child with an imaginary friend or to victims of trauma who retreat into religious fervour or magical thinking for a time. The notion that different realms exist simultaneously and that everything is both separate and unified is reassuring.

Firstly, it means that you are never alone: there are always others around you. For the Irish people it is (or, at least, was) curious, roguish fairy beings. Before dismissing them we should make sure that we truly understand what they were. To do this, let's first see what the Irish language can reveal about them.

We'll start with the words *Sí* or *sióg*, which are the principal words used for a fairy. *Sí* originally meant a burial mound (such as the Neolithic tombs) but then expanded to include the area around the mound and the magical beings believed to live in them, and it now also means a fairy, evident in the word 'banshee' (from *bean sí*, a female of the fairy world). But *sí* is also a common word for a gust or puff of wind, as in *sí gaoithe*. These words were previously unrelated; *síodh* meant 'burial mound' and *sidhe* meant 'gust of wind', but the standardisation of their spelling led to a belief that these gusts were the fairies scurrying by. *Sí* is pronounced like the English word 'she', and in fact also means 'she', as in the feminine third-person, singular personal pronoun *sí* ... but that's neither here nor there.

The word for 'peace' in Irish, *síocháin*, derives from the root word *síoth*, which is pronounced identically to *sí*. Indeed, in Scottish Gaelic the words for these are identical, with *sìth* meaning both 'fairies' and 'peace', which is curious, as fairy mounds were considered places of peace and plenty in which beings enjoyed long lives free from disease and poverty. It's similar to the image of paradise offered by Christianity and Islam, as well as by Hindu saddhus.

There is a similarity between the Old Irish spelling of *sí* (Old Irish *side*, Middle Irish *sidhe* or *sídhe*) and the Sanskrit word *Siddha*. These words have a common linguistic root: *Siddha* refers to an enlightened individual who has attained a higher spiritual state of consciousness, having divested themselves of the many worldly things that encumber the soul. This concept is common to Hinduism, Buddhism and one of the oldest known religions, Jainism. The latter regards *Siddha* as a wholly spiritual form of existence, without a physical body. This state is achieved by overcoming the desire for, and dependence on, earthly things.

Might that be a fitting definition of a fairy? Could the ultimate role of the Good People be that of an enlightened presence guiding us to the best path? Over the centuries their appeals to us to disengage from the trappings of human mundanity and connect with a grander vision may have been sullied, corrupted and confused, as happens often when people continually repeat a message without immortalising it on stone tablets.

Folklorists, including W.B. Yeats, believed that the fairy folk were gods during the reign of Tuatha Dé Danann but that, after we humans came along, they suffered neglect. In *Irish Fairy and Folk Tales*, Yeats quotes unnamed 'antiquarians' as saying that, 'when no longer fed with offerings, [they] dwindled away in the popular imagination, and now are only a few spans high'. This idea is supported by the poem 'The Hymn of Fiacc', which dates from the seventh or eighth century. Written in Old Irish, it may have originally come from the mouth of Fiacc himself, who was one of St Patrick's fifth-century apostles. The poem states that, before the coming of Christ to Ireland, the people worshipped beings called *Síde*. The 21st quatrain includes the line: *for tūaith Hérenn bái temel tūatha adortais síde.* In modern Irish this would be *Ar Tuatha na hÉireann bhí dorchadas, d'adhair an tuatha na Sí*, which translates as 'On the people of Ireland there was darkness; the people adored the fairies.'

If the Good People were once gods it is clear why they are dismissive of our earthly concerns. For them, time, space and all other human concerns are irrelevant. These little beings, who lurk beneath the bushes, in the trees and under rocks, watch on with an obsessive interest in the minutiae of our lives, yet they find it hard to understand our limited aware-ness and transitory obsessions. In fact with their pots of gold and magical potions they seem to be mocking our preoccupation with wealth and health.

That said, though the folklore often focuses on the mischievousness and short-tempered ire of the Good People, they tend to be benign and even helpful. They have lived here for thousands of years, long before we set foot here, and they are now generally bemused and bewildered by our trivial human concerns. There are countless tales of them offering cryptic advice to people, though this advice is often indecipherable.

Maybe the best analogy for the fairies is with Freud and psychoanalysis. Fairies are *seanchaithe* ('storytellers') guiding and prodding people's subconscious through magical stories about themselves, either stirring up or allaying hidden hopes, fears and biases that we'd rather keep under wraps. Most importantly, they connect people deeply with their environment.

Their message seems to be one of disattachment from human obsessions; we should instead follow their lead by dancing, feasting and taking it easy. It's a message preached by many sects and cults. One can regard the *Sí* as wise advisers, somewhere on the scale between Yoda and the Dalai Lama.

They can help us understand the Irish language in a deeper way, given how many words and phrases are soaked almost to saturation with references to them. You don't need to acknowledge them to speak the language, but Irish becomes richer and infinitely more nuanced if you do.

You can know that the Irish word for a security guard in a supermarket is a *foraire*, *faireoir* or *friothaire*, without knowing that the latter word (no longer much used) also means the senior lookout fairy at a fairy fort, as in *friothaire na rátha*. Or you can visit the Iron Age fort of Caherconree on a mountainside on the Dingle Peninsula without knowing that it is the reputed former domain of the superhuman mythological king Cú Roí, whose soul is said to rest in an apple in the stomach of a salmon.

Being aware of such things can't help but colour your outlook on the world. It's one of the reasons supernatural entities (which most traditional cultures identify with the land) didn't die out in Ireland. They were nurtured and nourished by the language ... and also by the unique relationship that Irish people have with the land itself.

LAND

We should talk more about land, and the best place to start is with *colpa*, a word that describes a certain amount of it. *Colpa* cannot be equated to 'acre' or 'hectare'; it is instead the size of a piece of land measured by its grazing potential. It was described in Eric Cross's novel *The Tailor and Ansty* (1942) as 'the old style of reckoning for land, before the people got too bloodyful smart and educated, and let the government or anyone else do their thinking for them'. It was carried into

Hiberno-English as 'collop', which Cross defines as 'the old count for the carrying power of land. The grazing of one cow or two yearling heifers or six sheep or twelve goats or six geese and a gander.'

Thinking about the term even for a moment makes you reassess your relationship with land. It's as human-centric as acres and hectares, but it manages to convey a sense of the ecological resilience of the ground. It requires getting to know a piece of soil, spending time observing it before laying claim to it – or to commodify it for profit.

It is this almost quantum quality of languages, particularly a native language, that makes them so potent and difficult to abandon in favour of another language – even for more practical, widely used and financially rewarding ones. It's also a quality that is hard to convey in the confined parameters of a language lesson; to appreciate it fully one needs to be outside, immersed in the landscape.

The idea of a *colpa* helps me reassess my essentially exploitative take on the 10 acres of gravelly drumlin I own in Co. Westmeath, and it makes me more aware of the ecological resilience of the soil, which can contend with no more than 20 pigs, 6 sheep and 4 hens, as I have found to my cost. But I am aware that the term still primarily conveys the extent and value of the terrain to human beings, as opposed to conveying its integral worth as an independent entity – as a natural patch of biosphere.

The principal word for 'field' in my Co. Kerry dialect is *gort*, and within this word are worlds of information that must be explored to truly understand what is being said. Its definition is a piece of land that can be ploughed by two oxen in one day, and if you've travelled through remote areas of Ireland, Scotland, Wales, Brittany or Galicia you intuitively know what a *gort* is and how it's different from an English field. You can probably picture its parameters and principal characteristics.

A key element is its boundaries, either a low wall of stones that have been painstakingly picked from the soil or else banks of sandy, gravelly, muddy or otherwise poor soil on which hedgerows have been planted or have naturally colonised. These linear strips of narrow woodlands, of which there are more than 350,000 kilometres in Ireland, contain up to 30 species, including hawthorn, crab apple and holly, depending on the environmental conditions. These strips were the natural apothecary from which herbalists collected their bounty. They are as much a part of a *gort* as the grass inside the boundary, or as the *pancán* outside, which is a bank in a field suitable for sitting on.

Within the concept of a *gort* is a system of co-operation and sharing of resources that we have now forgotten but may have to return to. Certainly the language has an idea of mutual dependence deeply ingrained within it. Our old system of law (in which the language is embedded) was based on the idea that households work cooperatively, forming annual mutual agreements to share resources in the form of oxen, ploughing equipment and manual labour.

The Old Irish word for ploughing is *comar* (Modern Irish *comhar*), which implies working in conjunction with other families. The verb makes no sense in the singular. To *comhar* on your own would be like dancing a solitary waltz.

Comar derives from the Proto-Celtic word *komarom*, which suggests that this practice of cooperative ploughing dates from before the first farmers reached Ireland. They must have brought it with them from where farming began, and while it's ancient, it was still widely practised when I was growing up in West Kerry. We'd all help to save the hay for a farmer if the weather was suitable on a particular day. At the time of my grandmother's youth on the Blasket Islands, the system was even more extensive, with families working together on almost everything, whether ploughing or weeding or harvesting, based on the central principle of *Ar scáth a chéile a mhaireann na daoine* ('Under each other's shadow is how people survive').

When practising *comhar* each partner could choose which field was to be worked each day, as long as the work (including moving the animals and equipment) could be done between dawn and dusk, which is why a *gort* is almost always clustered with other equally sized *gortanna* and also why they invariably have rounded corners, making it easier for a plough team to turn.

Again, all this is encoded in the word *gort*: the timelessness and the sustainability of the practices and the community bonds associated with them are all contained within it.

Yet, despite its elasticity, it would be hard to stretch its meaning to include the modern notion of a machine-moulded super pasture whose natural sustenance has been replaced with chemical fertilisers, whose insect life has been suffocated by slurry and whose diversity of herbs and flora has been replaced with genetically manipulated crops created in a laboratory.

The dictionaries have no choice but to extend the word *gort* to include this temporary freak of human exploitation, as does the modern Irish-language teacher, but it's a stretch. It's like saying that Nescafé is coffee or that a plastic gladiolus is the real thing. Maybe there will come a time when plastic gladioli are all that remains of this lily-like member of the iris family, by which time a *gort* will be the most suitable word to describe these bleak stretches of industrialised agricultural production, but for the moment the disparity is jarring.

FIELD NAMES

Of course, *gort* is only one word used to describe
a type of field and it is more common in my
Munster dialect than in other parts of the country,
where it tends to be used for a field of grown corn ...
as opposed to a field of corn grass, which is a *geamhar*.
What then of all the other types of field? Remember
*bánóg, biorach, machaire, buaile, inghealtas, domasach,
póicín, fásach, mainnear, réidh, cuibhreann, réidhleán,
cluain, mín, tamhnach, buadán, tuar, branar, plás,
raon, lóiste, plásóg* and *loscán?*

Those are some of the more easily defined words, but there are others, such as *cabhán, achadh, mothar, páirc, coimín, faicthe* and *áirleann*, which are more general. And there's also *mach, macha* and *magh*, which give us the word for 'outside', *amach*, literally 'to the field'. The notion of the principal location that one went out to was a field is a lovely thing.

To understand the subtleties of these words, we need also to be aware of their other meanings, such as how *losaid* and *lóiste* can mean a kneading trough or a table spread with food or how *cuibhreann* also means a partnership or association, as in the proverb *An té chaithfeadh boighreán i gcuibhreann an diabhail theastóchadh spiúnóg fada* ('He who sups with the devil should have a long spoon').

In my Kerry dialect the word *garraí* is used as widely as *gort*, but it refers principally to a field of potatoes, as in the great proverb recording the vegetarian's predicament: *Garraí le feoil is dhá gharraí le hiasc, is d'íosfadh an turaire an saol* (literally, 'A field with meat and two fields with fish, and the *turaire* would eat the world', the meaning here being that a single field of potatoes suffices when you eat meat; two potato fields are required if you eat only fish; while those who eat potatoes without any condiment would devour a world of them). Perhaps the best thing about this proverb is the word *turaire*, which means someone who eats food without sauce, meat or condiment. As an inviolate and unrepentant *turaire* myself, who likes to taste the quintessence of a thing, I value the fact that at least one language has bothered to give us our own name.

Looking at fields through the prism of Irish makes it clear how central they were to society. A *gort* was a priceless, almost sacred thing handed down through generations, having first been built up over centuries, sometimes by hauling seaweed from the shore to fertilise it; by burning limestone in kilns to enrich its alkalinity; by sending pigs in to root it up, cows to fertilise it and hens to condition the soil; and by having children pick stones out of it after each hard frost when the earth would disgorge ever more from deep underground. A *gort*, like a forest, was something begun by one generation and nurtured by the next in hopes that, in time, it would develop its true potential.

There was an understanding that it wasn't merely a unit of production: it was a living organism. In this view, more in line with an eco-logist's than with an agro-industrialist's, a field was a collective of biodiverse interactions, from the microorganisms labouring away on every leaf, stem and speck of soil to the miles of mycelium pulsating through the soil, connecting every atom in a natural network of unfathomable complexity.

The first time I visited the Céide Fields in Co. Mayo I looked out on a landscape of fields from five thousand years ago. I could see the barley ridges where our ancestors once cast their seeds in spring, knelt to weed in summer and harvested in autumn. It was humbling but also hard to grasp. The Neolithic cattle byres and burial tombs were clearly visible but it was the grain fields them-selves from a thousand years later, stretching out beneath the wild heather bogland, that most elicited wonder.

This experience was surpassed only by another set of field markings I saw recently on Achill Island, where I had been walking on Sliabh Mór (literally 'big mountain'), along the old potato ridges from the 1840s, left undug by local people when they realised that the blight had struck again and that the potatoes would be rotten beneath the ground. These ridges should have been flattened and dug again the following year, but by then the islanders were too weak to make it onto the hillside to plant a fresh crop, or else they had died or emigrated. As I was hiking through this area of tragedy and ghost fields, a local man showed me that, between the ridges, it was possible to make out a field wall from the Bronze Age. I could feel beneath my feet the unbroken tradition of working the land stretching back through eons. It's no wonder people sense something different in Ireland. The people have been rooted to this land, and to this language, for so long, growing grain, tending cattle, spinning stories. The continuity of tradition is closer to that of an indigenous culture than a European one.

This experience also emphasised the indelible nature of a field. Although humble and undistinguished compared with forests or cliffs, a field can last longer than any of the things listed in the old Irish proverb *Trí nithe is sia 'na bhfanann a rian: rian guail i gcoill, rian siséil i líg, agus rian suic i gcrích* ('Three things which leave the longest traces: charcoal on wood, a chisel on a block of stone, a ploughshare on a furrow').

In fact this proverb is itself an example of how elements of the language can leave lasting traces. It is from a collection of triads that the great scholar T.F. O'Rahilly (a cousin of mine whose father was the brother of The O'Rahilly's father) suggests date from the ninth century.

One great source of the history of fields is the names people have given them, which frequently reveal much about their topography, soil type, plant varieties, windiness, folklore and historical events associated with them. In recent years groups have begun collecting these kernels of knowledge. The Kilkenny Field Name Recording Project has managed to collate seven thousand old field names, of which more than a third are in various forms of Irish, even though the language hadn't been spoken in the area in several generations. The project curator, Alan Counihan, has noted that the

field names in Irish are those deemed most worthy of preservation by both landowners and survey volunteers. It is as though they offer pathways to an older time, to the life and language of our forebears, to the memory of a landscape and way of life that is threatened by the drive to higher productivity and the bureaucratic efficiencies that would rather record a field as a numbered block of pasture or an animal as a grazing unit.

Volunteers in Co. Meath have already gathered 24,700 field names. They regard them as 'the essential threads that hold that quilted fabric' of the landscape together. According to Counihan,

if we do not tend to its stitching the entire
weave will quickly unravel and the secrets
of an oral heritage handed down across the
generations will be lost forever.

A fine level field was the first thing that greeted a visitor arriving at a grand fort, according to the old sagas. This grassy plain was called a *faiche*, *áirleann* or *machaire* (all words still used today for smooth, even fields). It was here that people were assessed before being allowed to proceed through the stockade. It also served as a playing field for games and an exercise ground for troops, and it was the buffer zone between the hunting lands and the dwelling place. Wolves or enemies would first have to lope, charge or crawl across this area before attacking the fort.

Before we leave the topic of field words, let me give you four further field-related words, lest they be forgotten. The first is *faithcheacha*, which derives from *faithche*, noted above. *Faithcheacha* are voluntary contributions of food collected in the fields by what were known as the 'decent poor', who were ashamed to beg from door to door (unlike the 'delinquent poor'). The second is *scallach*, which refers to the singed stalks of burned heath standing in the ground, such as stalk ends in a stubble field. *Rianán* is a path across a tilled field and *domasach* is the light dry soil of a tilled field.

PLACE NAMES

The most direct and visceral way the Irish language is connected to landscape is through place names. While the local names for fields, hills, hollows, rocks, cliffs, trails and summits are enriching, it's the names of the 60,000 townlands that truly reveal the world around us.

Many of them are like koans, paradoxical riddles without a clear solution. They offer tantalising hints and encoded reflections of our culture, psyche and past practices that are becoming gradually less decipherable every year. There are glimpses into the historical, geographical and anecdotal qualities of our past just waiting to be revealed by those who understand the code. And now, with online resources, any of us can, with a little patience, begin to unpack them, just as one might unpack the pellet of a barn owl to reveal the husks, hairs and bone fragments within. By seeing beyond the archaic terminology and rare grammatical constructions, we can get tantalising insights into our ancestors' lives, their knowledge of environments and their folk beliefs.

In its anglicised form Bellanabriscaun in Co. Mayo means nothing, but Béal Átha na mBrioscán means 'the settlement of the ford of the wild tansy'. Suddenly an unassuming spot on a back road from Cong to Claremorris becomes a meadow rich with flat-topped yellow flowers smelling of camphor and rosemary. Images of the annual gathering of tansy that would have taken place there over centuries or even millennia are conjured up, with local people harvesting the plants to use throughout the year as a cure for joint pain and as a wrapping for meat, since its toxic compounds repel insects and maggots. A place like Bellanabriscaun would have received more covert night visits by women in distress, as tansy has long been used to induce miscarriages when taken in high doses.

Just south of the village of Adare in Co. Limerick is Knockfeerina, which was Cnoc Dhoinn Firinne ('Donn's Hill of Truth'). The name sparks curiosity, and further burrowing reveals that this was the power centre of Donn, a brother of Amergin's, the druid whose incantation propelled our world into being. (He was therefore also an uncle of Conall Cernach, who responded to the anguished wails of the shield Ochain by racing to do battle in Co. Armagh.)

It is said that Donn drowned with the rest of Amergin's family trying to reach the coastline but was later resurrected as King of the Munster fairies. He chose Knockfeerina for the site of his palace, from where he ruled over the rolling meadows of Co. Limerick, and he's buried there in a massive rock cairn at the summit. Local people will tell you that the truth, *fírinne*, referred to in the place name concerns the accurate weather predictions that certain residents of the area claim to make by gauging the appearance of the hill, but in fact it's connected to the deeper and more serious truth of life and death, represented by Donn's other persona, King of the Dead. The sight of his white horses galloping by on a stormy night meant that you were about to face the ultimate truth of your mortality.

Each place name is like a periscope, offering a view to another world, or another era. Carraig na nÓinseach (Carrignanonshagh) in Co. Waterford means 'the rock of the foolish women'. I could speculate on its meaning, but the mystery of its ambiguity is more appealing. In Co. Mayo there's a little inlet in Killary Harbour with a name simply too evocative to even attempt to decipher: Cuainín Ais-Sciorradh go hIfreann (Cooneenashkirroogohifrinn), which translates as 'the little harbour going back to Hell'.

It's hard to gauge what gets lost when we can no longer decipher these names. Does it matter that most people in Ballypitmave in Co. Antrim no longer know that they live in the townland of Queen Maeve's vulva (Baile Phite Méabha) or that those living in Skeheenaranky in Co. Tipperary may not know that their thorn bush, Sceichín an Rince, which was ideal for dancing, translates as 'the little thorn bush of dancing'?

How much value is there in knowing that Lisfarbegnagommaun in Co. Clare derives from Lios Fear Beag na gCamán ('the fairy fort of the small men of the hurleys')? Or that Lough Derreenadavodia in Co. Cork derives from Loch Dhoirín an Dá Bhó Dhéag ('little oak-wood lake of the twelve cows')? And what about Coosrinaneanwallig in Co. Kerry, which derives from Cuas Rinn an Aonbhallaigh ('the cove of the point of the solitary wrasse')? Why was there just one wrasse, and what did this solitary rock fish do to attain immortality in a place name?

The truth is that, over the course of millennia, we have developed these terms as our own way of relating to our surroundings. P.W. Joyce referred to it in *The Origin and History of Irish Names of Places* (1870) as a

great name system, begun thousands of
years ago by the first wave of population that
reached our island. [It] continued unceasingly
from age to age, till it embraced the minutest
features of our country in its intricate
network; and such as it sprang forth from
the minds of our ancestors, it exists almost
unchanged to this day.

Seeing the stoic promontories stretching out
into the sea like giant skulls, we called them *cloi-
geann* ('head' or 'skull'), and the term survives in
Hiberno-English as 'cleggan'. In the midlands those
dark-black sullen realms of spongy sphagnum mire
that vacillate between solid and liquid were labelled
bogach, meaning 'soft', which gives us the English
word 'bog'. The long ridges of post-glacial gravel
that rose above the bogs we called *eiscir*, which is
the origin of the term 'esker'.

In our place names the country is almost entirely
described through Irish. Over ninety per cent of the
names have their origin in the Irish language, and

a significant number of these are from before the seventh century, according to Dónall Mac Giolla Easpaig, former Chief Placenames Officer at the Department of Community, Equality and Gaeltacht Affairs. As P.W. Joyce noted,

> in our island, there was scarcely any admix-
> ture of races, till the introduction of an
> important English element, chiefly within
> the last three hundred years ... and accord-
> ingly, our place-names are purely Keltic.

The land comes alive through its place names in a way that those who cannot speak Irish will not perceive. A resident of Tandragee, Co. Armagh, who never studied the language will have no idea that Tóin re Gaoith means 'low lying ground near the estuary' and may be surprised when it floods in springtime. The name Feltrim in Co. Dublin becomes redolent when one knows that Faoldroim means 'the ridge of the wolves', just as Beenaniller Head (Binn an Iolair, 'headland of the eagle') in Co. Kerry makes reference to the eagles that once soared above it.

The writer and cartographer Tim Robinson captured this withering of geographical insight in his profound and elegant way in *Connemara: Listening to the Wind*: 'Irish placenames dry out when anglicised, like twigs snapped off from the tree.' The reality of this can be experienced in the Isle of Skye, where local people pronounce such place names as Sligachan, Galtrigill, Portnalong and Edinbane with no appreciation of what they meant.

Many Irish place names have been so corrupted by their enforced anglicisation that it can be hard to make sense of them, and they have been rendered into garbled and discordant forms: Ballymunterhiggin, Aghayeevoge, Ballywillwill, Treantaghmucklagh. These linguistically insensitive transliterations were done by scholars employed by the British Ordnance Survey during the 19th century, in the course of a programme to make improved maps as a way of reinforcing control of certain territories. It was a military strategy, a form of desecration – another violation heaped on the other humiliations inflicted on local people.

These maps present the world as perceived from the outside, rather than as the local people perceived it, personally and subjectively. Local people see their reality from inside – each one of us does, as does each community. The English attempted, however, an accurate but external documentation, losing the meaning of the names, which are a skin that one can pull on and inhabit. Theirs was a cursory accounting of the land more than an attempt to convey its full visceral interiority.

It should be noted that the scholars employed by the English surveyors were Irish. They were aware that their superiors wanted names that approximated the pronunciation of the Irish names and, as the work was being done during the 1830s and 1840s, during the height of the Famine, they may have thought that Ireland's future lay in embracing the English language and its wider world. Repeated bouts of starvation had made it clear that their Irish culture was at an end and that their survival depended on abandoning the old ways and embracing the foreign culture. The money they earned for their work may even have been going towards preparing their children for exile.

And so we are left with etymological jokes like Muckanaghederdauhaulia, in Co. Galway, which sounds like a fable land in a nonsense poem but derives from Muiceanach idir Dhá Sháile ('pig-shaped hill between two seas') and Faslowart in Co. Leitrim, from Fás Lúghoirt ('deserted herb garden'), which sparks the question of how and why it was abandoned.

Rather than the loss of the wolves in Feltrim, of the eagles at Beenaniller, of wild boars of Kanturk, Co. Cork (from Cionn Toirc, 'headland of the wild boar') or even the leprechauns at Mullenlupraghaun (Muileann na Luprachán, 'mill of the leprechauns') near Cong, Co. Mayo, it is actually the loss of this Co. Leitrim herb garden at Faslowart that most gets to me. What happened to it and to the woman (for it was invariably a woman) who tended it? And to her knowledge of the culinary and curative powers of those herbs? Although this book focuses on the amount of knowledge we still have about our past, one of the most gaping holes is our knowledge, or even awareness, of the medicinal plants and fungi that were once used. The most powerful women healers were protective of their wisdom, and this was compounded by the fact that scribes, who were almost all men, may never have thought to ask them.

DECIPHERING PLACE

The English conquerors regarded Ireland's place names simply as a mass of incomprehensible sounds, but we know from the *Dinnseanchas* that the Irish people saw them very differently. Topography was so central to Irish tradition that it makes a word like *Dinnseanchas* almost impossible to translate. The nearest one can get is 'the lore of notable places', but this fails to capture the countless layers of memory contained within each place name and how the tales connected to them convey the influence that place names have on the people and animals living within, or visiting, the space. The nearest equivalent term might be the Tjurunga lines of the Aboriginal people of Australia, often called 'songlines' or 'dreaming tracks', that summon the land to life through songs that are sung along invisible trails in the landscape.

At its most potent, *Dinnseanchas* has a similar ability to manifest elements of the landscape into being, or at least alter our perception of the environment so that our minds read the land on a more profound and unfettered level. It's a complex, illogical, intuitive lore that often appears to be absurd or fanciful.

For the druids a central motivating factor was the preservation of the collective memories of the tribe. This was paramount, as their allure and authority as historians, spell-casters, storytellers and genealogists depended on the tribal memory remaining intact through the generations. Their legitimacy stemmed from their knowledge of the long-distant past.

This is recognised in a passage in the Senchus Mór, an ancient text said to be the first attempt to transfer Irish oral traditions to writing. It consists of a recording of ancient laws as modified by the introduction of Christianity. A section of it poses the question 'What is the preserving shrine?' and replies to itself in the manner of a Socratic dialogue: 'Not hard: it is memory and what is preserved in it.'

In a world before writing, or any other recording system, memory was the bulwark for maintaining a sense of identity, of tracing lineages of spiritual or military leadership, of tracking patterns of climate change and vegetation growth, of collating and conserving cures and remedies. To 'know' the world meant to memorise it.

The Senchus Mór emphasises this point by repeating the question 'What is the preserving shrine?' and using the same rhetorical flourish to answer: 'Not hard: it is nature and what is preserved in it'. It is conveyed that even more reliable than the human mind for maintaining the ancient memories is the natural world. The land holds memories within it. This is a challenging idea to us now but it was pervasive in ancient thought. It is essentially an articulation of the soul of place.

Each significant location in Ireland had a story about how its name came to be associated with it. The *Dinnseanchas* is therefore a neat symbiosis of memory and land. It can be hard to decipher this facet of it now, as the tales have been tainted by medieval fabrications added by later storytellers or scribes. There is also the issue that we have forgotten how to unpack the complex truths often hidden within far-fetched tales. By extracting the wisdom and memories contained within a place name through a mix of analysis and intuition, we can cast light on profound truths about people, gods and nature.

In fact the simple act of telling the stories of place can help root us back into the biosphere of a locality that stretches back through time. For example, Loughanleagh is now an unassuming hill in east Co. Cavan between Bailieborough and Kingscourt. Parts of it are covered in heather and gorse but most is now blanketed under dense plantations of spruce and pine. Hearing that its name in Irish is Lochán Leagha ('the lake of the physician'), and that it was renowned for its cures, starts you on a journey of discovery that can transform the place and your sense of the world.

Firstly, you notice that there is no longer a lake and you wonder why. More careful observation shows that there are three species of heather growing here and that these reveal healthy, ancient peatland underfoot. This suggests that this was once a wetland area that has been dried by the introduction of ditches so that the peat could be extracted as fuel.

But what about the cures that were in the lake? A local person will talk of ancestors who were healed of scurvy, shingles and mumps by the lake's waters, and they will explain that later the mud from the bottom of the lake was considered so powerful against rosacea and even leprosy that it was sent to far distant parts.

You will also hear about a goatherd named Peggy Dunt who helped bestow supernatural abilities on the lake during the era of the Penal Laws in the 17th and 18th centuries. Peggy was out tending her goats when she spotted English soldiers coming from the direction of Moybolgue, and she immediately began filling her apron with stones, which she collected not to fire at the soldiers or to drown herself in the lake but to throw at the goats so that they would rush down past a priest who was illicitly saying mass on this remote hillside and would have been executed if caught.

The priest, realising that the goats were a warning, hurled his chalice into the lake just before the soldiers arrived, and he was then able to blend in among the parishioners, who pretended that they were merely out picking fraughans, or bilberries, still plentiful in the area. It was this chalice that bestowed the curative powers on the lake, a local tells you, but it's clear that the lake's magical ability stretches further back than that.

The prehistoric rock cairns heaped on the three highest points of the hill reveal that this site is far older than the Penal times. That Peggy collected the stones in her apron reveals that this is a more ancient tale, as this image is a trope of ancient stories about Irish witches and goddesses. In fact Loughanleagh is mentioned in the mythology of the Neolithic ritual chamber at Loughcrew in Co. Meath, where the great witch, a *cailleach*, gathered stones into her apron and flew across to Co. Cavan to drop them there to form the three cairns on the hill.

A local person will tell you to look out for St Patrick's knee mark on a rock near where the well of the lake was; on your next visit you will find it and will clearly see an indentation carved into the stone in the shape of a rough horseshoe, but because it faces towards the rising sun over Dundalk Bay it is likely that it too is far older than St Patrick. It's a remnant of a ritual of our sun-worshipping ancestors.

And so an area of seemingly bland upland spruce forestry is transformed into a spot of pre-historic ritual devotion, of magic cures, of Catholic defiance and, most visibly, of the environmental impact that human action, such as turf-cutting, has on the landscape.

Through a place name we get to renew or enliven the land and revitalise our relationship to it. It focuses our attention on the now absent lake and all the flora, fauna and heritage that went with it. We become sensitised to the countless species of animals, lichens, insects, trees and microbes that were nurtured by and at Lochán Leagha and at its well and surrounding peatland. And it makes us look more closely for lingering reminders of it.

And when you do look around again with this new awareness, you will suddenly spot a sedge patch stretching out over half an acre, and you will notice it's a little lower than the surrounding land. In an instant you will realise that it is there, the ghost form of the once-magical lake. You'll have embedded yourself in the landscape and the ancestral timeline to such an extent that the invisible will become visible. You will become linked to a place in a way that is the polar opposite of our current sense of disconnection and alienation from our surroundings.

THRESHOLDS

Maybe the best way to understand place names is to see them as thresholds – as portals through which you can access other eras or access the Otherworld that was always only a thin veil away. Just as a place name represents an opening into a wormhole of insights into the history, archaeology, landscape and fauna of an area, they also lead us through to the world beyond, from which everything initially emerged.

To fully appreciate this idea we need to understand that the Otherworld was more than an imaginary realm where the ancient gods and heroes dwelt and feasted; it was an elusive and indefinable space that was as much connected to the subconscious or inner psyche of the individual and the group consciousness of the community as it was to magical gods, or the spirit of past ancestors, or the energetic resonances of the natural world. All these things come together in the Otherworld, just as they might in a dream, and place names became just another way to access them, like using sacred trees or rituals or charms.

There's a tale of a man in Lochán Leagha, Co. Cavan, who was out hunting at dusk and spotted a hare on the hill. He was just about to kill it when he noticed that it had a massive red eye in the centre of its forehead. He realised it was some form of supernatural being, most likely a wise woman or goddess, as they frequently took the form of hares. He watched transfixed as she leapt into the water and dived back into the Otherworld, where she belonged. It was from this knowledge – that the lake was at one time an entranceway to the supernatural realm – that its curative powers arose.

The most famous threshold point in Ireland is probably the passage tomb at Newgrange in Co. Meath. Nowadays it is a major tourist site, with countless coach tours and a sprawling interpretative centre. It is here that the great god of the sun sends down a beam of light at the winter solstice every year. The light penetrates a long stone passage to light up a womb-like space beneath the earth that was built between 3200 and 3100 BC. Its modern Irish name, Sí an Bhrú, itself becomes a threshold between the modern world and the multitudinous layers of history and divine intervention that occurred there from time immemorial.

Sí, as we've already seen, means 'fairy mound', and *an bhrú* means the hostelry or fairy palace, so Sí an Bhrú means the fairy mound of the hostelry. However, Irish-speakers reared in folklore are likely to be familiar with some of its alternative names, such as Brú Mic an Óg (the living place of the god

Daghdha and his son Aongus) and the name of the wider Megalithic complex, Brú na Bóinne ('the fairy palace or hostelry on the Boyne River'). These alternatives are all encoded within, or behind, the main place name – like rooms beyond a front door.

On one level Sí an Bhrú can be used as a utilitarian term in postal addresses or road signs, but it can also be a springboard to all sorts of dizzying peregrinations through mythological labyrinths. The English name, Newgrange, contains none of this, instead channelling a different story. A 'grange' is an outlying farm belonging to an abbey or an estate, and the name Newgrange arose when this land was acquired by Mellifont Abbey in the 13th or 14th century as an additional farm to feed the monks.

The word 'Boyne' (Bóinn) itself requires unpacking. It stems from a goddess named Boann who was married to Nechtan, the guardian of a sacred well of wisdom in the Otherworld. Only Nechtan and his three male cupbearers could approach the well, and when Boann attempted to do so she approached from the wrong direction: she had walked the opposite to *deiseal* ('sun-wise'), which is how one should always turn when engaging with the natural or spiritual world in any meaningful way, such as casting a net, winnowing grain or performing a ritual. To protect itself the well rose up and washed her away, and in the process she was badly injured, causing her to lose an eye, a leg and an arm, thus limiting her sight and her movement in this world.

The waters then chased her to where the mouth of the River Boyne is now, and she died there, her body becoming the river that we know today. There are many thresholds hinted at in this account: the well is a threshold to the Otherworld; Boann's damaged eyes are a threshold to the visible world; and her body then becomes a long, aqueous threshold in the physical world to the goddess that exists beyond.

There are countless other stories about Boann, many contradicting each other, such as that she represents the Bó Finn ('White Cow'), a mythical maternal being, and that her gushing waters are a physical manifestation of divine milk that nourishes the land around her. It's a grand example of the bewildering murkiness and hazy glimpses of deeper insight that are encased within the *Dinnseanchas*.

The key is to bear in mind that words in Irish, and particularly names, were not just composed of an arrangement of symbolic letters from an alphabet on paper. In fact they never existed in this form within the oral tradition. They were pure sound, more like an embodied medium, and they could be communicated only by vocalising them into the surrounding air from within the cavity of a physical body. In this way words were embedded in the human body and the physical senses to an extent that is legions away from these digitally processed words on the page that now enter your mind with virtually no physical transference. The dissociation and disembodiment of writing and reading are an apt metaphor for our increasing alienation from the sensual, natural world that place names capture so well.

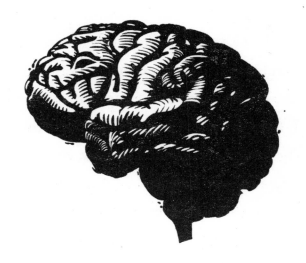

IRISH SONGLINES

It would be wrong to overemphasise the similarity between Aboriginal Australian songlines and *Dinnseanchas*, but the former can help cast some light on the latter, in that an indigenous Australian with knowledge of the songs and of the appropriate sequence in which they should be sung can navigate vast distances, even across the most inhospitable deserts. Some songlines are short, while others are unimaginably long, but if you know how to decipher them they will reveal the landscape around you, offering information about the myriad species of animals and plants, including their characteristics and behaviour throughout the seasons and through different weather patterns.

What songlines amount to is ultimately a functioning map of a location that can help steer the singer between waterholes, landmarks and other natural phenomena. Often it is the signs left behind by the Creator on the land when the physical world was fleshed into existence that are highlighted in the songs, so that one finds evidence of the formation of islands, rising sea levels and other ancient landscape changes recorded within the words. Similarly, many of Ireland's *Dinnseanchas* tales arose from marks or rock formations left by ice sheets, post-glacial floods or Neolithic inscriptions etched in stone up to eight thousand years ago by the first settlers.

And just as the *Dinnseanchas* contains information beyond the mere alphabetical symbols of the words, songlines too must be comprehensible beyond the initial meaning of the words, as they span the lands of tribal groups that speak different languages and have varying cultural traditions. They are therefore created so that the most important information is communicated through the sound and melody. Their rhythms echo the contours of the land, and their beats mark out the footsteps of the ancestors so that they transcend the limitations of conventional language.

This idea of binding memory and information to place and movement is now a commonplace of socio-geographical seminars and TED Talks at which motivational speakers wow audiences with their ability to receive, store, process and recollect memories by employing similar techniques. In 2014 the Nobel Prize for Medicine was awarded for research that unearthed cells that constitute a positioning system in the brain, establishing how closely memory and spatial awareness are intertwined in the hippocampus. The finding confirmed the pairing of place and memory evident in songlines and in the *Dinnseanchas*.

WITCHES' HILL

Speaking of threshold points such as Lochán Leagha and Newgrange, I should mention the one that has had the greatest influence on me, which is Loughcrew, a prehistoric ritual site in Co. Meath, just up the road from my home in Co. Westmeath. This is the site that the *cailleach* created by dropping rocks from her apron onto the sheep-grazed hills of Carnmore East and West. At first the land appears to be nondescript undulating pasture, but closer investigation reveals an extraordinary collection of ancient ceremonial sites, Neolithic works of art and some of the oldest free-standing buildings known.

I was reminded of these features when I was examining the patterns on the speaker on which I had spread flour to assess the vibrations created by spoken language broadcast on the radio. The designs and decorations appearing on the black paper from the sound waves were remarkably similar to the water spray pattern from an *isréada*, a wooden switch used to sprinkle holy water over boats, crops or cattle for protection. The droplets rising into the air from the *isréada* and outwards in swirling arcs and starbursts were believed to transform the essence of any object they landed on in a beneficial way.

As I played a recording of the ancient poem 'Cailleach Bhéarra' ('Old Woman of Beara') through the speakers, the grains of flour began shifting into an arrangement of concentric circles, zigzagging lines and radiating forms that reminded me of something I had seen etched onto a stone buried in an underground chamber at Loughcrew. When

I made the connection I jumped straight on my bike and headed up there, past dilapidated cottages, new bungalows, old graveyards, the ruins of an aristocratic mansion and two medieval lime kilns, towards the pair of green bellies that rise in gentle undulations from the landscape.

On my way up the steep hill of the main Loughcrew mound, I passed a council worker trimming the grass in semicircular arcs against the direction of the rising sun. It reminded me of Mick Tobin, who had tended these grass banks with a scythe until his death a few years ago. It was he who told me about the concept of *deiseal* ('sun-wise'). It's the direction of mindful approach, as the goddess Boann found to her cost when she came on Nechtan's well *tuathal* ('anti-sun-wise'). Mick said that plants grew *deiseal* so that one had to cut them *tuathal*.

I'm not sure if the council worker's trimming against the direction of the sun was done instinctively or if it was something he'd picked up from his elders, as over the centuries *deiseal* has acquired such potency that it has become a form of blessing. You say it when someone sneezes or has eaten something that went down the wrong way, to ensure that things go right for them.

As I mentioned earlier, my grandmother taught me the need to orient myself in relation to the sun when speaking Irish. Instead of saying 'I'm going over there' or 'back home', she would have me give compass bearings: I'm heading *soir an bhóthair* ('eastwards along the road') or *ó dheas* ('to the south'). It's as if we are heliotropic plants ever focused on the sun.

When I was a child I was once locked out of our house in Co. Kerry, and a neighbour, Maidhc Idá (the man who told me that the clay pipe I found in the ground was a *pipín lutharagáin*, 'leprechaun's pipe'), saw me struggling at the door and called across, *Cas an eochair in aghaidh na gréine* ('Turn the key against the sun'). I had no idea what he meant and continued to flail at the lock until he came over and turned the key himself, repeating the words as he did so. The door swung open as if by magic, and I thought his words had worked as some form of incantation, given that it had seemed impossible to open a moment before. I just couldn't wrap my head around the idea of matching the sun's orbit to that of a cylinder in a lock.

As I grew older I learnt to adjust my sense of space quite significantly during the months I'd spend in the Gaeltacht each year, as things could become indecipherable if I didn't remain attuned to my position in relation to the sun and the wider cosmos … although some more vague expressions to indicate location are now becoming common, such as *thall ansin* ('over there') and *suas an treo sin* ('up that direction').

Mick Tobin maintained that one must always go *deiseal* around Loughcrew when approaching the tombs. This was the direction the *cailleach* flew in, he said, and in which the great planets turned. I was impressed by this notion of us and the planets turning in the same direction towards the sun, until I recalled that the Earth revolves anticlockwise and that the planets of our galaxy and of surrounding galaxies spin in various directions.

When I pointed this out to him he just reached for his whetstone and began sharpening his scythe, skating the stone in sunwise crescents along the iron blade until it was sharp enough. He looked up then and said:

Sure, I know that, and the folk who designed those tombs knew that too. It's just that sometimes it's better not to overcomplicate things. Them lads long ago working out the solar alignments of these places or the lads in NASA putting satellites up in space need to contend with such matters, but for the rest of us there's no great need.

I continued on up past the trimming worker towards the primary earthen mound of Loughcrew, which is part of a complex of more than thirty chambered cairns clustered over three peaks. These are the remains of what was once a vast and complicated Stone Age ritual site, positioned directly between the ceremonial monuments of the Boyne Valley to the east and Carrowmore, Co. Sligo, about

110 kilometres west. It's a heady place, with the remains of corbelled passage tombs scattered across the hills. These are decorated at significant points with now-indecipherable symbols – a profusion of concentric circles, zigzags, swirls, radiating lines and coiled curls.

I went straight up to the top of the highest mound, known as Cairn T, which was once cloaked in white quartz, and looked out at the grand sweep of land stretching over 18 counties in all directions. It's one of the few spots in Ireland from which all four provinces can be seen, but the focus of the site is primarily on what lies beneath. For under this mound of stone is a dark passageway lined with massive boulders leading towards a series of small chambers marked with sacred symbols from five thousand years ago.

I clambered down from the rocky mound towards the entrance portal, which is flanked by two guardian stones; but before entering into the belly of the earth, I retreated ten steps northwards to a massive ten-ton rock that directly abuts the base of the cairn so that I could approach the entrance on a *deiseal* rotation.

This rock is known in English as the Hag's Chair, because a protruding edge, reminiscent of armrests, was carved into it thousands of years ago. There were also cup-mark symbols etched into the face of it that are largely eroded now, but the principal feature of the rock is that it points directly north. Sitting in the throne at night you are looking straight out at the Pole Star – a reminder that the entire site is oriented from the underground plane burrowing into the earth to the horizontal plane of the surface ground stretching out to encompass the widest vista of Ireland, and then onwards up into the vertical plane of sky and universe beyond.

The entrance to the cairn has been painstakingly positioned to ensure that the morning sun of the spring and autumn equinoxes shines directly down from the sky plane through the earth plane and into the ground along a descending passageway, illuminating a decorated stone in the back chamber. Not only this, but I've heard amateur archaeoastronomers claim that the layout of the cairns and tombs mimics the Auriga constellation and that its location is perfectly aligned with the sixth brightest star in our sky, Capella, which is 42 million light years away. This is only hypothesis, and may more accurately be described as a flight of fancy, as could the theories that the tomb's entrance points directly at Sirius and that the cairns are positioned purposely under the supermassive black hole that is the rotational center of the Milky Way.

In fact the role of the Milky Way in the minds of Irish-speakers is worth considering. The Irish name for it is Bealach na Bó Finne. The word *bó* means 'cow', and *bó fhionn* is a pale or white cow. *Bealach* means a road or trackway. But, as we've heard, *bó fhionn* is also another derivation from the name Bóinn, the Irish name for the River Boyne. It also refers to a mother goddess who bestows her bounteous nutrition on the world.

Now, this river and goddess are bountiful with flowing milk or water and are so luminous at night that their light is reflected into the sky to form the

Milky Way, which is why it's called Bealach na Bó Finne. Furthermore, the sacred tombs and passage graves – such as Newgrange, Knowth and Dowth in the valley of the Boyne – were believed to be arranged in relation to galactic constellations of the Milky Way so that the sky is reflected onto the land, just as the land is reflected into the sky. All of this is encoded in the name Bealach na Bó Finne.

CIRCLES

From the Hag's Chair, I passed through the guardian stones and into the tomb of the principal Loughcrew cairn, feeling immediately the visceral disorientation we get when air and light are replaced by damp earth and wet stone. The dark cavern had a thick and clammy atmosphere that made me want to retreat, but I continued onwards, feeling my way along the musty rocks, crouching down as the roof seemed to drop lower in places before rising again.

I then tripped on a boulder marking the end of the passage and the entrance to the inner chamber. I landed on my knees in this sanctum, which is roughly the width of a shovel, and there was a ritual altar and a stone basin on each side. For a moment I stayed on the ground to catch my breath, feeling the familiar sense of claustrophobia and intense focus that the space always brought me.

I first heard about Loughcrew while travelling through the Himalayas almost two decades before. I had been trekking towards the Nepalese border when I came across a meditation cave on the lower slopes of Nanda Kot that had been used by many hermits over thousands of years. A Brahmin priest came out to welcome me and explained that he was there for the winter, having retreated from his life in Varanasi to seek deeper connection with the Earth. When he heard where I was from he said that there were extant places like his cave in Ireland too. I nodded politely, not wanting to correct him or to explain that the Irish people now worshipped in churches, not caves. He didn't press the point, only patiently asking me what Hindu gods I knew.

'Krishna and ... Kali.' After pausing a while I remembered Vishnu too.

'The word "Krishna",' he said, 'does it remind you of anything?'

'Christ?' I said.

'Yes, but anything in your own language, in Gaelic?'

I was surprised he knew about Irish but attempted to think of something similar. 'Well, *crios* is the Irish for "belt".'

He shook his head. 'I'll give you a clue. Krishna comes from the Sanskrit root "Krish", meaning "existence" or the "core essence". Does that help?'

I thought for a long time before hesitantly saying, *croí*, which means 'heart' or the centre of something.

He nodded, smiling. 'The root of the word "Krishna" can be traced forward and backward through many languages that spring from the same source. At one time we shared the same gods, you know? You mentioned Kali, the goddess of war.

Does she remind you of anything in your language?'

'Well, *cailleach* is a wise woman or a hag,' I said. 'It's similar to "Kali".'

Delight spread across his face and he replied, 'And I read that in Ireland there is Sliabh na Cailligh, which has a cave very much like this one.'

His words didn't mean anything to me at the time. It was only years later that I bought my 10 acres in Co. Westmeath and discovered that the Loughcrew cairns were just up the road. On my first visit to Loughcrew I noticed the signpost: Sliabh na Cailligh (with Cailligh pronounced 'kali').

I remember that first time edging my way into the cavern, just as I was doing now, with my arms outstretched, shuffling forward on my knees through the gloom, feeling my way further underground to where my fingers could feel the faint imprints on the rough damp stone that forms a back wall of the chamber. This is the stone on which the early-morning sun at the spring or autumn equinox sends its beam of light shooting through the portal and down the passageway to land here and trace a pattern across the engravings in the rock. At every other time the stone hides in darkness, waiting for those rare few mornings a few times each decade when the sun is not hidden in clouds.

These are the rare moments it communicates. Otherwise, it stays silent and hidden. It reminds me of the many words in Irish that are seldom said aloud but remain in waiting for their moment to shine, such as *peicín* (the froth of porter collected in some insalubrious pubs and mixed with fresh liquor), *loisideach* (abounding in kneading troughs) and *bróis* (whiskey for a horseman at a wedding). They lie dormant until someone somewhere decides they are needed to convey the specific idea they represent.

I switched on my torch and was bathed in a brightness that revealed the gritty pockmarked rocks that form this tiny inner chamber and its bewildering jumble of coded markings, as enticing and indecipherable as a child's sketch. These markings were familiar and alien at once. My brain immediately tried to make sense of the curves, spirals and dots, and sometimes I seemed about to decode a particular pattern of a field, flower, sunbeam or snake – but then everything would get jumbled and bewildering again. This was a form of communication in Ireland before Irish developed. It was the precursor of our current language.

Yes, the Brahmin was right that Irish stems from Indo-European roots that can be found in Sanskrit, but there may be vestiges of this potentially pictographic language of the stones buried within the Irish I speak today.

It was the circle patterns that sparked an association when I was examining the flour patterns on the speaker. The same spiralling motifs were carved here into the rock, suggesting celestial orbits and seasonal sun patterns. It brought to mind the word *beacht*, which means a circle, a ring or an assurance but is also the principal word for 'precise' or 'perfectly'.

Loughcrew was all about calculating precisely the circular orbit of the planets around the sun and the assurance that, after the bleak descent into winter, spring would come again and with it a time to plant seed. The sun would send its shaft of light through this pillared birth canal into the womb of the earth at the spring equinox to illuminate the stone and warm the earth for planting.

I recalled then that *beacht* is also a way of conveying the concept of 'for ever', as in the phrase *go beacht*, and that a further meaning of the word is 'meditation'. That was when I started staring harder at the circular shapes that are the foundation of so much of Irish culture – evident in everything from the rounded buildings and ring forts to the bowls, butter churns and brooches. In fact it's hard to think of anything that had a square edge for thousands of years in Ireland, despite the efforts of Vikings and Normans to introduce rectangular buildings and objects.

The old word for a rounded house was a *clochán*, which could also mean a collection of houses or a village or an unofficial burial ground. But its original meaning was a druidical circle of stones for pagan worship. And I thought about the fact that I was here in a circular mound that had been constructed more than five thousand years ago, with quartz rocks that had been carried hundreds of kilometres over land and then hauled up here. All around me were satellite circles in the form of smaller cairns positioned on circular hills, and to access them I had to follow linear routes, like the trails of meteors shooting between planets, or like the bonds between atoms. To access the circular and spiral carvings hidden within the circular cells of these cairns, I had to cut through linear passage-ways that bisect the circle. The whole space was geometric, arranged around this notion of concentric circles and their relationship to planets and stars and orbits.

To put it concisely, or *go beacht*, I had entered a world that was more closely aligned to the galactic or sub-atomic fields of reality than the conventional, rational world we like to believe we inhabit, and I couldn't decide if this was exciting or disconcerting.

RESONANCE

I had emerged from the cave at Loughcrew for some air and to get my bearings, for the place always disorients me a little. Sheep were huddled behind the shelter of the entrance stones, and in the distance I heard the bellowing of a cow. It was a very particular call – an unmistakable sound that, once heard, can never be forgotten. The Irish word for it is *diadhánach*, which means 'lonely', though it's a particular form of loneliness: that of a cow bereft of her calf.

If you've ever heard a cow lowing at the loss of her calf, you'll appreciate the effect of *diadhánach*, as our bodies tend to respond empathically to it. The keen goes straight to our hearts, and intuitively we feel a sense of her despair and the strength of her desire to be reunited with her baby. All of this is packed into *diadhánach*, and by stopping and considering it we become connected more deeply to the world around us. It's a good example of how words can be wedges that prise back the surface layer of thought and feeling, revealing a deeper truth.

Feeling the tug in my body from the anguish of that cow made me think about why sounds can resonate so clearly inside us. This idea of resonance in language is something important in Irish. Lubhdán, king of the fairies, is described in a medieval text as having *guth gluair áib uma*, a 'voice clear and sweet as copper's resonance'. Copper, *uma*, was referred to because it is the metal used in the finest sacred bells for its strong tone and ability to maintain clear resonance. It provides the quality in the bell that makes you stop and turn inwards, just as the lowing of a cow does.

This reminded me of research that archaeologists have conducted into the resonant properties of caves and cairns. With their corbelled ceilings, stone baffles and indented niches, caves and cairns have some of the same features that are now built in to acoustically engineered concert halls, which, after all, are only modern versions of caves and cairns. I had read that cave paintings in France and Spain from twenty thousand years ago were often situated in the precise spot where the finest acoustics were to be heard. In fact archaeo-acoustic researchers regularly discover new paintings by moving through the pitch darkness of a cave while singing until they reach a spot where the acoustics are particularly resonant. Once in position they shine their lights on the walls. Often they find an image there, and even if the wall is too rugged, flaky or damp for anything to be made out, the location will be marked with a few painted dots.

But none of this got me any closer to understanding what had so captured me about the flour patterns on the loudspeaker. I wished I could have brought the speaker with me or at least have it on video so that I could compare it to the carvings directly. I headed back into the cairn at Loughcrew and began chanting random words into the space, singing them out loud once or repeating them over and over, simply because it felt good to do so. *Loisideach, bróis, peicín ... Loisideach, bróis, peicín ... Loisideach, bróis, peicín ...*

I noticed a slight echo when I directed my voice at particular points, and without thinking I realised that my random words had melded with those of the poem 'Cailleach Bhéarra', which I had played through the speakers. The poem describes the travails of an ancient land goddess who conferred sovereignty on kings and brought forth winter each year. But to give you a sense of it I need to tell you a little more about this *cailleach* who lived for centuries, going directly from crone to young girl, just as winter shifts to spring. She outlived seven husbands, and her children, grandchildren and great-grandchildren went on to create whole races of people. It was she, the poem states, who created Loughcrew by dropping rocks from her apron, as she had done at Loughanleagh in Co. Cavan.

Finally, in the sixth century, when Christianity was established in Ireland, she realised that her time was up, and she surrendered her pagan powers. Or at least that's what the monks recorded in their chronicles about her. Once she had lost her powers and agreed to wear a veil as a sign of submission, she became a wizened old woman, loudly lamenting her glory days to anyone who'd listen – reminding people of the freedom and vigour they all once had before succumbing to Christian doctrine.

Her words are preserved in a lament later committed to writing. The earliest version is from the ninth century, though, of course, it's far older. It's long and rambling, but my two favourite verses are the ones I found myself reciting into the walls of the rock caves that she had created.

A-minecán már-úar dam;	I am cold indeed;
cech dercu is erchraide.	every acorn is doomed to decay.
bith i ndorchuib derthaige!	to be in the darkness of an oratory!
Rom-boí denus la ríga	I have had my day with kings,
oc ól meda ocus fína;	drinking mead and wine;
in-díu ibim medcuisce	now I drink whey-and-water
eter sentainni crína.	among shrivelled old hags.

The more I sang the more impactful the sounds around me became, so that in time I could feel the reverberations as the sound waves crossed my body, passing through it, almost. It was eerie but invigorating.

I turned off my torch and stayed squatting there in the darkness, chanting away to my heart's content, pausing only to catch my breath now and then. I realised that the space was ideally suited for chanting, and I noticed that the sounds echoing at me were different from those that had come from my mouth. They had a different resonant frequency, and I wondered if that was why these places were said to alter consciousness, as I knew that altering resonant frequency can affect the brain and body, as well as the general surroundings.

Research in a similar chambered mound in Orkney in Scotland shows that, by creating resonant frequencies with human voices inside a cairn, one can make a massive stone block outside shake with such vigour that the vibration is evident to bystanders. Another cluster of Scottish cairns at Camster Round, Caithness, were somehow acoustically interlinked. A person drumming inside the cairn could not be heard from outside, yet the sound appeared inside the neighbouring mound of Camster Long, which was at least twice as far away as the area outside the cairn, and there were no tunnels or air channels between the two cairns.

In 1994 a group from Princeton University led by the physicist Dr Robert Jahn tested the megalithic chambers at Loughcrew, Newgrange and three sites in England. The group found that the chambers could all sustain a strong resonance at a frequency of about 110 hertz, which is the tipping point that sparks altered patterns of activity in the prefrontal cortex. This frequency causes the language centre of the brain to deactivate to a degree, and it causes a shift from left-sided dominance to right, the side related to emotional processing.

The easiest way to create this frequency is by singing – which makes it possible, or even likely, that the space was designed for chanting, with some of the standing stones positioned to enhance the chamber's acoustic properties. Perhaps they were later retro-fitted to 'tune' the natural resonance to the required frequency. The right words said at the right pitch in such a space could activate an area of the brain that behavioural scientists believe relates to mood, empathy and social behaviour.

After I had been chanting for some time, I was so addled that I could have sworn that the sounds were coming from inside my own head rather than from my mouth. The Old Woman of Beara had her grip on me. There was also the possibility that I was being affected by infrasound, which is beneath the threshold of normal human hearing – a little below 20 kilohertz. Such sounds can be felt, if not heard. The sound of drums and other musical instruments contains infrasonic components that researchers have shown are enhanced inside chambers like the one I was in.

At the resonant frequencies I was hearing, even small shifts can produce significant changes in volume, because the acoustic system stores vibrational energy. Echoes bounce off the rocks and compound before they fade. Laboratory testing has shown that exposure to these frequencies affects the brain. People who use more of their frontal lobe will experience a shift in how they receive ideas and thoughts – similar to what happens during meditation – while those who favour the back lobe will see more images. Would the effect have been different if I were chanting in English? Certainly the frequencies would have been.

I realise that all this may sound rather far-fetched and tangential to the Irish language, but in fact we can't fully appreciate Irish without realising that our ancestors believed that the sounds themselves had the potential to alter their surroundings.

Archaeologists are now studying the practice of bringing seeds to such chambers to perform rituals on them and 'activate' them before planting. Tests of ancient ritual structures in Mesoamerica have found that corbelled chambers, like those at Loughcrew, have a measurable effect on seeds. The structure of the space increases certain electrical anomalies, with positive ions sinking to the floor and negative ions rising, resulting in a measurable pulsing within the chamber. This electromagnetic variance, when replicated in a laboratory, can influence the viability and productivity of seeds. On-site trials in similar chambers in New England have shown that indigenous seeds germinate earlier, grow faster and produce heavier yields after undergoing this process. It is not known whether a similar practice existed in Ireland, but seeds of staple crops appear in large number within Irish caves.

SOUND

I't's hard to say anything definitive about the effect of sound on the world, but we all recognise that it has some influence. The Huygens Principle, discovered in the 17th century, explains why two clocks with pendulums ticking in proximity fall into rhythm with each other, resulting in a single ticking sound. The beat of both clocks is set at 1 hertz (that is, one cycle per second), and as they radiate their ticks they force each other to harmonise.

In a beehive, each bee's sound varies according to its age: very young bees fan their wings at 285 hertz; adolescents fan at 225 hertz; and older bees fan at 190 hertz. But humans simply hear a note of E3, with a variance that descends a perfect fourth and ascends a half step. If our ears could differentiate these frequencies we could perceive much additional information encoded within them. Electronic monitors can trace frequency shifts that the bees make when different threats, opportunities or issues arise in the hive. It's a form of communication that can be deciphered even by human ears if they are trained to perceive the subtly varying frequencies.

The effects of these sounds on the bee colony is considerable and instant. The presence of a toxic chemical will change the sound within 30 seconds, with as many as 30,000 bees altering the vibration of their wings almost in unison. Researchers have identified particular frequencies the bees emit in response to certain chemicals or other danger. It's like a biological alert system, with a unique audio signature to communicate each threat.

Scientists are also finding that, though most humans can't differentiate these frequencies, the frequencies nonetheless have a physical effect on us. The humming causes cerebrospinal fluid in our brains to resonate. This fluid provides basic mechanical and immunological protection to the brain and the spine. It also circulates nutrients and filters chemicals from the blood. Sound frequencies not only stimulate this fluid but also affect the pineal gland, the pituitary gland, the hypothalamus and the amygdala. And, of course, it's not just the frequencies of bees humming: certain words and phrases, when said in the right way and in the right context, have a similar effect.

Druids and poets were all too aware of the power of sound, of how sounds can directly affect our bodies and surroundings. Old poems draw attention to places with particularly resonant or attractive soundscapes. In one section of Agallamh Oisín agus Phádraig ('The Colloquy of Oisín and Patrick', a series of poems that survive in their earliest written form from the 17th century but are likely to be older) Fionn mac Cumhaill's son, Oisín, reminisces about the wonder of the nature-based world, as opposed to the new, authoritarian, doctrinal era of Christianity. In this translation by Eleanor Hull, Oisín lists the harmonious sounds of forest and shore that predominated before the arrival of the human-made noise of bells and prayers.

> The blackbird's pipe on Letterlea,
> The Dord Finn's wailing melody.
> The thrush's song of Glenna-Scál,
> The hound's deep bay at twilight's fall,
> The barque's sharp grating on the shore,
> Than cleric's chants delight me more.

We see a similar focus on beneficial sounds in an ancient triad listing the three best sounds in the world: *fuaim an tsúiste, fuaim na brón, agus fuaim an luinithe* ('the sound of the flail, the sound of the quern, the sound of the churn-dash'). Another triad lists the three sweetest sounds as *meilt bhró, géimneach bó is béic linbh* ('the turning of the quern, the lowing of a calf, the call of a child').

Unless they are onomatopoeic, words cannot convey a particular sound, but Irish does try to capture certain sounds by allocating specific words to them. *Uilg tuilg* is a sound uttered in moments of sorrow or defeat, and *húrla hárla* is the roar uttered in moments of elation. The sound of a clanging bell was rendered *gricc gráicc*, with *gráicc* being the word to describe the braying of a donkey or the croak of a raven (perhaps implying that Irish bells weren't made from the finest resonant copper but from a cruder form of metal). *Mingur gringur* seems to have been the buzzing or humming made by insects, *fo-dhord* being specifically the murmuring of bees.

All these sounds moved out into the world in the form of vibrations that consisted of wave forms, as we've seen. And we're very familiar with how waves affect our lives, even though we can't see most of them: solar waves from the sun; short waves to a radio; high-frequency waves from loudspeakers or in microwaves, rippling through our food, heating it by vibrating the molecules.

There is nothing unusual or esoteric about waves having an effect on us, and words affect us the same way. When words emerge from our vocal folds, pushing the molecules in the air back and forth as they radiate, they affect the medium through which they travel, whether that is air, water or our physical bodies. Irish, which has been spoken by our people for millennia, resonates in specific ways as it emerges from us and passes through us.

I certainly feel like a different person when speaking Irish. It's possibly how a fingerling feels when becoming a trout, or a nymph becoming a dragonfly, or a grasshopper becoming a locust. It's hard to imagine the previous version of myself from within the new form.

ARABIC

I have mentioned that Irish has linguistic connections with India. This is in need of further elaboration, but let's begin with how Irish is potentially connected to Arabic …

Muinín in Irish means 'confidence' or 'trust' or to be hopeful that someone will do something. The Arabic word for this is *mwinenh* (at least, that's the word used in Oman). *Gearradh* is the Irish for 'cut'; in Arabic it's *gyarra*. *Caladh* is the Irish for 'port'; the Arabic is *kh'ala*. In Malta I heard *shkupa* used for 'brush', and it sounded enough like the Irish *scuab* for me to ask its derivation. I was told that it was a Maltese Arabic word. Throughout Yemen and the Middle East, I've heard *sakin* and *sikina* used for knife; in Irish it's *scian*.

What's going on here? How could Arabic have ended up in Irish? Does the English word for the national symbol, the shamrock, derive from an Irish word (*seamróg*) that came directly from the pre-Islamic Pagan Arabic *shamrakh*?

For the answers to all this we need to investigate the origins of the first settlers on this island. They can now be traced back six thousand years to a multicultural swathe of the Middle East known as the Fertile Crescent. A migration of later Mesopotamian farmers merged with the island's original settlers to form us.

We can touch one of these early farmers, or at least her bones and skull. These were dug up in Ballynahatty, near Belfast, and analysed by the geneticist Dan Bradley at Trinity College, Dublin. Having fully sequenced her genes, he found that she 'possessed a genome of predominantly Near Eastern origin' and that 'she had some hunter–gatherer ancestry but belonged to a population of large effective size, suggesting a substantial influx of early farmers to the island.'

A forensic sculptor has reconstructed her face in accordance with the evidence, and she appears to have had a high forehead, black hair, brown eyes, a button nose and a compact, sallow face. Sadly, she can give us no clue as to what language she spoke 5,200 years ago, but it's possible that some of the words she uttered are, after much mutation and change, still embedded in the Irish language of today.

The world of DNA evidence is still in its infancy, but it's already been upending everything we thought we knew about ourselves. It now appears that the people who built the passage tombs at Newgrange, Knowth and Dowth were not us. The genetic lineage between them and us is not continuous. This makes the type of vague leap of conjecture that I'm attempting here all the more challenging. The ancestries that a people imagine for themselves can be just as important as their actual ancestry when tracing the transfer of shared material culture and common practices.

The latest revelations from DNA records chime with the synthesised accounts of our origins found in the 12th-century manuscript Lebor Gabála Érenn ('The Book of Invasions of Ireland'), a collection of far earlier accounts of the history of Ireland and its people from the creation of the world to the Middle Ages. It is a semi-mythological account of the settling of Ireland but the narrative that can be distilled from it is that the settlers were Celts from the Iberian Peninsula and that their coming to Ireland took place over a long period and in several migrations. The progenitor of the Irish people, it states, is Míl Espáin, who came from the Middle East to conquer Spain, his sons later continuing on to Ireland. This pattern of migration is similar to what Prof. Bradley is finding in the DNA, and this assertion of Middle Eastern and Arab influence is suggested in other ancient Irish texts.

For example, in the stories preserved in 'Accallam na Senórach' (an 8,000-line poem from the 12th century) there are descriptions of arabesque designs on warriors' shields, and references are made to musical instruments having an 'Arab style'. In fact this Arab style may be evident today in the tendency in Irish traditional music to roll notes on a flute or fiddle or in *sean-nós* singing to an almost exaggerated degree. It's remarkably similar to the rolling and swirling notes in Middle Eastern music and of doing the same with sounds while singing.

Taken on its own this would be merely a coincidence (though the Arabic resonances in *sean-nós* cadences are uncanny), but the same tendency is evident in the elaborate decorations that cover every inch of free space in the Book of Kells. These too are reminiscent of the elaborate swirling decorations that typify the arabesque ornamentation covering the walls of mosques or, in later form, of Alhambra palace in Granada.

It was the filmmaker and historian Bob Quinn who most conspicuously sought to examine connections between the Irish and Arab worlds. The similarity between the sails on a traditional Connemara boat, the *púcán*, and on the Arab *dhow* or *felucca* on the Nile, sparked his curiosity, and in the 1980s he set off on a long journey of discovery that resulted in his book and film *Atlantean*, which dared to suggest that Ireland might owe as much to Arabia as to Europe.

In Morocco he found a stone carving from the second century BC of a figure surrounded by a wavy serpentine line, with a series of overlapping, concentric half-circles etched on top, which reminded him of the entrance stone to Newgrange. He then noticed the same coiling, serpentine motif throughout Ireland and on stone carvings and rock art up along the coast of Brittany, Galicia, Portugal and the Berber regions of North Africa.

Then, in Msoura, a region of Morocco between Tangier and Rabat, he stumbled on a megalithic circular mound composed of 167 standing stones surrounding a tumulus almost 55 metres in diameter. The highest monolith in the formation was a 5-metre phallus stone, identical to one at Punchestown, Co. Dublin, and similar to one documented at Newgrange in 1699. Either Neolithic people in the Boyne Valley and North Africa simultaneously developed the classic passage tomb in the form we know it today, or there was contact between them.

In fact we've known since 2006 that there were relations between the Irish and Arab worlds by AD 800. A psalter was dug up in Faddan More bog, Co. Tipperary, containing 60 sheets of vellum inscribed with the Book of Psalms from the Old Testament. The cover of the book is lined with papyrus that came from Egypt, and the cover itself may even have been made in Egypt by Coptic monks.

Seven hundred years before, the Greco-Egyptian astronomer and geographer Ptolemy, who lived in Alexandria, was able to glean enough information about Ireland to list its geographical features, including its principal rivers and even the small island of Lambay off the coast of Co. Dublin. This island happens to be one of the many Irish sites, alongside Croghan Erin in Kiltale in Co. Meath and Belmullet in Co. Mayo, at which archaeologists have found tombs of people buried standing up, as is the practice in parts of the Middle East.

It should be no great surprise, then, if Arabic has left a mark on our language, or vice versa. The continents were far more connected in the past than we imagine. The journey by sea across the Mediterranean and up the Atlantic coast was easily achievable in either a *púcán* or a *dhow*. In fact in favourable winds it would have been faster, safer and more reliable than many far shorter journeys over land – even than crossing the central bogs and forests of Ireland.

What is also surprising is that the concept behind Ireland's national emblem, the shamrock, may have been imported from Persia or elsewhere in the pre-Islamic world. This preeminent symbol of Ireland may in fact be an import.

Legend has it that St Patrick used the shamrock to illustrate the doctrine of the Holy Trinity, which led to its being used as a national symbol.

This might be true, but if so it's interesting to learn that the people of the Arabian Peninsula in prehistoric times worshipped a trio of goddesses known as Manat, Al-Uzza and Al-Lat and that their symbol for these goddesses was the three-leafed *shamrakh*. The word *seamróg* is a diminutive of *seamair* (clover), so the similarity may be a coincidence, or else early Christian missionaries brought knowledge of a plant with symbolic attributes from the Arab world and applied it to the white clover, wood sorrel or lesser yellow trefoil that they found in Ireland.

Either way, it cautions us to regard anything as being unique to a particular culture. Instead of regarding our language as being in some polarity with English, we should see it as a living remnant of a form of communication that has been used for millennia across swathes of Eurasia. Accordingly, the poet Gabriel Rosenstock has argued that Irish could be adopted as a lingua franca of the European Union as it is one of its earliest languages.

We could regard it, perhaps, as the language of the 'people of the Atlantic seaways', as Bob Quinn suggests, but if so we must bear in mind that these Atlantic people were connected to those in the Mediterranean and that from there merchants could reach the Red Sea and Arabian Sea overland through Egypt. They could also reach the Asian subcontinent by boat along the ancient Canal of the Pharaohs that connected the Mediterranean to the Red Sea via the Nile in various periods of pharaonic history stretching over 2,500 years. Nothing was ever isolated: everything was interconnected.

As Irish-speakers we should regard ourselves as members of a unified cultural archipelago of coastal people who have more in common with each other than with the centralised powers that control them.

INDIA

The idea of Irish being just another expression of the many tribes that have converged and diverged over millennia is strengthened when we look at the Hindi language and Indian culture. If the links between Irish and Arabic seem redolent, just wait till you see those between Ireland and India. I could begin with examples of uncanny similarities between Irish and Hindi words, but let's skip ahead to why two such seemingly distinct and distant cultures might be enmeshed in this way.

The most widely held hypothesis, based on linguistic, archaeological and genetic evidence, is that a large mass of humanity, known as the Indo-European peoples, migrated west to Europe and south-east to India from a central area between Russia, Ukraine and western Kazakhstan, bringing their common language and beliefs with them. Other arguments are that our shared ancestors spread out in different directions from Asia Minor (now Turkey), Armenia or India. The point is that one can track so many similarities between the cultures of India and almost all of Europe that we must have been very closely linked at one time.

But that doesn't explain why prehistoric links between India and Ireland might have remained stronger and longer than between India and the rest of Europe. The most likely explanation is that both are on the margins – Ireland to the west and India to the east – and while change tends to happen fastest at the centre, the edges continue on without succumbing to each new influence.

Somehow the Celtic world (which had its roots in a common tradition shared with India) survived in Ireland for hundreds and even thousands of years after it faded, or was extinguished, in continental Europe. So, for example, our stories talk about the caste-based system of society that we once had – a system that can still be seen in India today. The highest caste were *aire* ('nobles') in Ireland, while in North Indian society they were known as *aryas* ('noblemen').

In India the king (*raja*) ruled with the help of local Brahmin judges who applied the law, and in Ireland the king (*rí*, from the same Indo-European root word as *raja*) ruled with the assistance of Brehon judges, who were the lawyers of Celtic or Gaelic Ireland. Their laws, known as Brehon Law, contain numerous parallels with India's Lawbook of Manu. The word 'Brehon' is an anglicisation of the Irish word for judge, *breitheamh*, which stems from the Indo-European root word *brih*, meaning 'master of mantras'. *Brih* is also the root of the Sanskrit and Hindi word *Brahmin*.

So, in social structure we see parallels, but they are also evident in systems of belief. Before the Brehon Laws were fully set in place, legal matters were settled by the druids, who also oversaw the spiritual leadership of the people. An explorer from Asia Minor named Dio Chrysostom commented in the first century on how similar Celtic druids were to India's Brahmins. And it's hard not to notice striking similarities between certain examples of Celtic spiritual art and ancient Indian images. For example, a Celtic deity, Cernunnos, a horned god of fertility, is frequently depicted sitting in lotus position with an Indian-style headdress and meditative gaze. He looks uncannily like depictions of the Indian god Shiva, and there are other carvings of Celtic sages posed in meditative postures like a yoga guru.

The druids claimed that their ancestors were Tuatha Dé Danann, the supernatural tribe of earth-bound gods. Their name translates as the 'people of the god Danu', with Danu being the name of their goddess, most probably Anu or Anann. Anu was an ancient river goddess throughout Europe, but you'll find her in India too, where the Vedic mythology refers to a race called the Danavas, who were the sons of Danu, and in their culture Danu is connected with the waters of heaven.

So, both cultures trace their lineage to these followers of Danu. There's a great account of their arrival in Ireland in a poem in the 12th-century Lebor Gabála Érénn ('The Book of Invasions of Ireland'), which describes them as coming here riding in 'flying ships' surrounded by 'dark clouds'. (Of course, the poem is far older than the 12th-century manuscript it is recorded in.) They landed on Sliabh an Iarainn ('Iron Mountain') in Co. Leitrim, where they 'brought a darkness over the sun lasting three days'.

The Irish for 'druid' is *draoi*. In Old Irish it was *druí*, with the genitive form, *druad*. It stems from two Proto-Celtic words whose roots have parallels in Sanskrit, *dru* and *vid*. In the earliest forms of Irish the word *dru* meant 'immersion' or 'total connection'. It also referred to the oak, specifically to a sacred tree of life whose central trunk ran through the middle of the cosmos, keeping the sky aloft. The topmost point of this tree was the North Celestial Pole, the one static point in the northern heavens that all other stars circle around every 24 hours. In India this pole, or world axis, topped by the North Star, was called *dhruva*. It is akin to the role that the spine plays in yoga, being the central axis of the body through which all energy and wisdom flows.

The word *uid* or *vid* meant knowledge. *Oideas* still means 'knowledge' in Modern Irish, while in Sanskrit the closely related word *veda* means the same thing. So, a *draoi* was one immersed in knowledge or a knower of the world axis. It was his responsibility to keep track of the sun, moon and stars that circled the celestial axis so that important religious festivals could be celebrated at the right time of year.

There are numerous other similarities between druids and Brahmins. Each represented the religious and learned classes of their societies, and they shared a belief that truth was the life-giving and sustaining power of the universe and that oral memory, in the form of poetry, was the best way to sustain sacred writings and histories, even after they developed the ability to write. But there's probably no need to labour the point. It seems likely that Gaelic and Hindu culture are manifestations of the same spiritual and cultural past.

These things are rarely acknowledged in Ireland. Few Irish-speakers consider that our primary saga, Táin Bó Cuailnge, is focused on cattle droving, just as India's principal epic, The Mahābhārata, is – and that our tales contain many of the same motifs and themes.

Had I not met that cave-dwelling Brahmin two decades ago I might not have thought about it either. He had asked me what the Irish word for 'saint' or holy man, and I told him, *naomh*.

'In Sanskrit it's *noeib*,' he said.

It was a freezing day on that Himalayan mountain and the snow was falling heavily and settling thick on the ground. I was keen to continue on my way, to reach the village of Munsyari on the Nepalese border by nightfall.

I tried to move off again, but he said, 'To

express the idea of wish or prayer, we say *mánman*. Do you know this word?'

'It's the Irish for "mind",' I said, 'and for "thought" and "desire".'

'Interesting,' he said, 'because in Hindi it also means "thought" or "desire".'

'*Meanman* is actually the genitive form,' I said. '*Meanma* is the nominative.'

He smiled beatifically, his eyes twinkling. 'You see a pattern?'

I wondered if he had been an academic before giving up everything to follow the sadhu's life.

'Even our god Govinda,' he continued. 'You know Govinda? He's a manifestation of Krishna. He is the same god as your River Boyne.'

'I'm not sure you're right, there,' I said. 'Boyne comes from *bó fhionn*, meaning "white cow". It's nothing to do with Sanskrit.'

He just smiled. '*Go* is the Sanskrit word for "cow". 'So, *go*, *bó*. They are both gods offering nourishing life-force goodness, sustaining their people with the flowing milk from the divine cow.'

Maybe Irish people don't focus on these things because the implications of it all unsettle us. That idea that Irish and Indian societies are like two mirrors reflecting back at each other beyond time and space is bewildering. It's far easier to focus on more recent colonial connections, such as Irish words like *seampú* ('shampoo') and *bungaló* ('bungalow') that come via English from British soldiers during the time of the Raj.

The Brahmin went on to tell me that the *vinda* in Govinda comes from another word shared by Sanskrit and Celtic languages, *uind* ('find out' or 'know'). It's related to the early Celtic word *vindos* ('white'), as in the name Fionn, the name of the goddess Bó Finn and the Welsh name Gwynn.

But let's return for a moment to the word *draoi*, and its root, *vid*, meaning 'knowledge'. Its most common use in Hindu culture is in the word *veda* – the plural of which is *vedas*, the name for a collection of hymns and other ancient religious texts written in Sanskrit between 1500 and 1000 BC. The word *veda* is interpreted as 'the knowledge' or 'the word'. It represents the essence of the divine principle that is the fundamental building block of reality. By reciting Vedic mantras Hindus believe they can help strengthen reality, which is in a process of entropy or constant decay. Vedas are like a blueprint for the universe: they can call forth reality through annunciating elements of the primal sound that existed at the moment of creation.

Reciting Vedas is a way to ensure that reality itself is perpetuated – all other benefits of mantras are secondary to this. It is similar to reciting the *Dinnseanchas* to keep the landscape alive or to Amergin's incantation manifesting the Ireland of today.

The Vedas that you might hear being chanted today in Hindi or Sanskrit are likely to be diluted examples of what went before. Some people claim that they used to be more primal or guttural, and this seems possible, judging by the example of some isolated clans of Brahmins who still perform ancient fire rituals in remote forested areas of Kerala. Here, in the course of ceremonies that continue for days, they chant Vedas and mantras that appear to be in no discernible language; their closest parallel in sonic patterns is birdsong. These sounds are impossible to write down and can be passed down only orally through generations. They appear to be the roots of the sacred chants used today – words that were not above meaning but beyond it.

It is this attribute that spiritual leaders refer to when they talk about how the ancient sacred languages of the world (such as Hebrew, Sanskrit, Sumerian and Mayan) preserve trace elements of early primal sounds and invocations within them. Encoded within these languages are elements of the belief system of the first humans to develop speech. In the right mouths they can be vessels of revelation. If this is true it should be no surprise that Irish, with all its similarities to Sanskrit, might also be capable of conveying some of these attributes of continuity and communion with distant epochs.

THE CURE OF WORDS

As it happens, Irish-speakers have always acknowledged that some sounds within the language have a potency beyond the literal meaning they convey. My grandmother knew a woman in Limerick long ago who would call to a house if she heard there was a child there with mumps. She'd loom over the bedside, staring at the bed a while, breathing in the smell of the child before heading out to the hen shed, where she would incant *A kark, a kark, kut an leka shuh.* She'd repeat this a few times, despite having no real idea whether the words meant anything, as she didn't speak Irish. It was simply what she had been taught to say. She believed in their power and the fact that they had always worked for her. *A kark, a kark, kut an leka shuh.*

An Irish-speaker will recognise that what she said was *A chearc, a chearc, chugat an leicneach seo.* ('O hen, O hen, take on these mumps for yourself.') Every child she uttered these words for was cured within a matter of weeks. Of course, the body can cure itself of mumps naturally within that period, but they believed the power that was in the sounds.

Could this have been similar to Amergin summoning up our world through his words, or is it more likely an incidence of the practice of trans-ference that is still found among indigenous people in South America and Polynesia? The language becomes a vector or a medium through which to transfer the illness to another animal or inanimate object by some magic words or act.

In Ireland, if the spell didn't work there was another option, which was to put the blinkers of an ass on a sick person and lead them to the river to drink – directly with their lips in the water rather than from any vessel. Ideally, also, the current should be running southwards to carry off the evil.

Even among those who do not speak Irish, the language was deemed particularly suitable for these types of spells. In parts of England, if a person or animal swallowed an insect, there was a custom of singing 'Gonomil, orgomil, marbumil, marbsai, ramum, tofeth' into their ear (right ear for men and boys or male animals, left for women and girls or female animals). To English people the words were meaningless, but an Irish-speaker can decode them. They are saying, *Goin an míol, airg an míol, marbhaigh an míol* ('Wound the beast, harass the beast, kill the beast').

Another example of this is the charm for curing an enlarged prostate gland, which appears to be in neither Old Irish nor Modern Irish but in a mix of Middle Irish and Latin. *Dumesursca diangalar fúailse, dunesairc éu ét, dunescarat eúin énlaithi admai ibdach* ('I save myself from this disease of the urine, and from salmon envy. Save us, cunning birds, bird flocks of witches, save us').

I remember my grandmother telling me about the ailment called *an cléithín*, for which I still haven't encountered an English equivalent. It has to do with the displacement of a small piece of cartilage at the lower end of the breastbone. According to the custom, the way to cure it was to place a cake of uncooked oatmeal dough on the belly and stick a candle in it. Then, after warming a glass in the candle, you placed the glass directly on the skin. You'd see the sucking effect on the skin as the glass cooled. This has nothing to do with language, except that the only translation I knew for *cléithín* is as a diminutive of *cliath*, 'wattle', which is a framework of branches woven together and used to make fences, gates, beds, walls, doors and also known as a 'hurdle'.

Cliath can also mean other things, such as the splint for a hen's leg, the treadles of a loom, the darning of a stocking, and a tool to keep a poultice (such as the cake of uncooked dough) in place on a body before safety pins. It can also mean a harrow and a plate and a raft. The Irish name for Dublin, Baile Átha Cliath, means 'the settlement at the ford made of hurdles' (for crossing the river), and in Old Irish there is the term *Clíatha Fis*, which some sources claim were beds on which druids lay to access supernatural knowledge.

These wattle beds were used by druids when all other means of divination failed them. They would lay out fresh bulls' hides on wattles of hawthorn branches to sanctify or imbue them with the wisdom of this sacred bush. Then they would wrap themselves in the hides and go to sleep, hoping to absorb the wisdom of the hawthorn overnight. So, someone who is said to have gone *ar a chliathaibh fis* ('on his wattles of knowledge') is considered to have gone to great lengths to access information.

One old text imagines the process for using the *cliatha fis* as being *luidhset na druidh fora cliathaib fis 7 rothoghairmset demhna 7 dei aerdha na n-docum*, which in Modern Irish would be *luigh na draoithe ar a gcliatha físe agus tháinig deamhain agus déithe aertha chucu* ('the druids went on their hurdles of knowledge and summoned to them demons and aerial gods').

Clíatha fís would have made a great term for the internet: it means a 'matrix of knowledge'. It would have chimed with the word for 'spam', *turscar*, which also means the washed-up refuse of rotten seaweed and shellfish found on the shore. *Turscar* is almost as resonant as the Cherokee word for email, *anagalisgi gowelv*, which literally means 'lightning paper'.

But back to cures. There's one listed in the Stowe Missal, a Mass book of the early Irish church written mostly in Latin. The cure is half in Old Irish and half in something else entirely – possibly the last remnant of a language that was spoken here before Irish ever reached the island. Maybe it is just gobbledegook that was intended to make it sound more cryptic and potent, like how doctors call an ingrown toenail *onychocryptosis* or call the headache you get from eating ice cream *sphenopalatine ganglioneuralgia*. The words of the charm are *Fuil fuiles camul lind lindas gaine rath reththe srothe telc tuse lotar taora muca inanais behad nethur* … No one has been able to translate it fully, but it seems to begin with the advice to 'Put the urine in … your … and your health …'

Here's one final charm to show that the right Irish words said in the right order can have remarkable results, even if they are not completely intelligible. The following was found in an old manuscript in the National Library of Scotland. The catalogue records it as being a 'charm to protect the vulva'. The charm is *'Bir bran ar leor meor'*, *scríb so an slait caotrainn* ⅂ *cuir fo cosib mna* ⅂ *ni fathar banndacht*. This can be translated '"*Bir bran ar leor meor*", write this on a rowan branch and put it under a woman's feet and she won't suffer from female troubles.' The words *bir bran ar leor meor* appear to be Irish, but it is hard to say what they mean. Their meaning evidently wasn't as important as the effect they would have when written on a stick and stood on.

WOMEN AND
WITCHES

It was almost always women who dispensed these healing words. Certain of them had access to spells and esoteric ways that remained a mystery to most, and this is the aspect of Irish culture that was lost earliest and is hardest to reconstruct. The medicinal and herbal lore of women was almost never written down, and the most accomplished practitioners tended to be marginalised and treated with caution. They didn't dare record their knowledge, and mainstream society never dared to ask or wasn't interested. Still today there are a few women left with some knowledge of cures and remedies, although there are precious few of them and their knowledge has diminished considerably.

It is hard to say if anyone now knows how to cure a *brat* (a film on an animal's eye) by treating it with hare's blood. (*Brat* can also mean the covering placed over a ewe's quarters to prevent a ram from covering her; a swathe of hay; a cloak; or several bags sewn together and put under corn when threshing.) Who now knows that a *sleamhnán* (a sty in the eye) was treated with a poultice made of bread and cat's urine? Or that *fuílleach fíréid* ('ferret's milk') was a cure for whooping cough, or that the only way to milk a ferret is to use a *préaslach*, which is a bit, gag or rod secured in a ferret's mouth?

People no longer know how best to store a *bodalach* (part of a calf's intestine hung up in a chimney and kept as a cure or for greasing boots, although it can also mean the paunch of a fat man, a large cow's udder or an ungainly youngster). There is possibly no one left who knows the difference between it and *Tadhg an Gheimhridh*, which (as far as I can gather) was meat stored in the rafters and then taken down as a cure.

In a library in Bailieborough, Co. Cavan, there's a small ring-bound folder that contains a list of folk healers, with a listing of which supposed cures they could perform – whether dealing with warts, tuberculosis, skin cancer or Bell's palsy. There are only a few men listed in the notebook; the majority are women. Their speciality is listed alongside their phone numbers or an address. The notebook might date from the 1970s. How many of these healers, if any, are alive today? There's an entry for a woman with the cure for hiatus hernia in the townland of Crookswood, and there are instructions on how to find her.

Go on to filling station, take left turn, and
then left again past school, into narrow
lane, half mile, lane on right. Through gate

house in wood (niece lives at end of lane).
——— is an elderly person. Generally works
Sat-Mon-Thurs.

The power these healers were believed to possess made people uneasy and so they tended to live isolated lives. One could regard them as the last vestiges of the *cailleach*. I have already translated this as 'old woman', but it can also mean a wise woman or a sorceress. Its original meaning is closer to a veiled woman or a nun. In songs *cailleach* tends to mean a precocious or licentious girl, but in poetry the meaning sticks closer to the idea of an unpleasant old woman, or a woman who doesn't follow convention and so wields unusual power.

That a *cailleach* is almost always imagined as wearing a *caille* – a veil – is significant. There was mystery to her. As a child in West Kerry, I saw on one or two occasions isolated women who seemed immersed in their own worlds and who were treated with a mixture of deference and wariness.

In mythology the *cailleach* was the personification of winter and so her veil may have represented the land being clad in frost and snow. In Scotland and the north of Ireland her method for hastening winter was flying and beating back the summer vegetation with her cudgel. The Irish word for this implement is *farcha*, which also means a maul, mallet or thunderbolt. She'd stir up strong winds or set the sea spewing by belting the sky and the earth. Her primary impetus wasn't so much malevolence as a wish to agitate, to incite change – an awareness that things require an animating force. All this information is encoded in the word *cailleach*, and Irish-speakers would be aware of much of it and would be considering certain aspects each time they used the word.

There is another range of meaning for *cailleach* that may stem from her secondary role as a guardian of herds and food stores through the winter. *Cailleach* can refer to a small alcove for storing your knitting or your pipe, or to the recess in a wall for a bed, or to a snug in a bar. Along the same line of things that protect and safeguard, *cailleach* can also mean an anchor made of stone or the butt of an old tree that lasts for decades. But mostly it's a decrepit, withered thing, including a shrivelled potato or a worn shoe.

There is often a certain sinister sense to the word – of a black-clad, veiled, otherworldly figure, which in Irish is now connected with other ominous slow-flying beings, like the owl, which is sometimes referred to as *cailleach oíche* ('the night witch') and the cormorant, sometimes called the *cailleach dhubh* ('the black hag'). In fact in parts of north Co. Mayo the word 'cormorant' is not used by older English-speakers. 'Kaillek duv' is the only term they use for it.

The best-known *cailleach* was Cailleach Bhéarra ('Old Woman of Beara'), whom we've already encountered. She was said to be the daughter of the little sun of winter, who is born ancient and grows younger and more powerful as the days shorten and the sun weakens, until eventually, at the advent of spring, she transmogrifies into a vibrant young maiden named Brigit. It's wrong to regard this winter queen of storms and death as an enemy, because she has within her the vibrant, life-giving essence of Brigit, the spring goddess.

That's some concept for a single word to encompass. One almost needs to take a pause to process it all. We're deep into the rabbit hole already, but there's more meaning that we must contend with, namely how old the *cailleach* is. A Scots Gaelic poem, dating from a time when Irish and Scots Gaelic were practically the same language, suggests that the *cailleach* is so old that she remembers a time before the Atlantic Ocean was formed, when the landmass of Ireland was still connected to the Appalachian mountains in America. The poem is 'Cailleach Bheag an Fhàsaich' ('Little Cailleach of the Wild'), and in it she states: *D'uair bha an fhairge mhòr 'na coille choinnich ghlais, bha mis am mhùirneig òig* ('The time when the great sea was a grey mossy wood, I was a young girl').

This line may sound fanciful, but the Atlantic Ocean was indeed once a wooded landmass that was torn asunder when the supercontinent

Pangea was broken up by shifting plate tectonics. Ireland was on the Eurasian plate and was separated from the North American Plate. That's why the Blue Ridge Mountains of Kentucky and the Appalachians of the Carolinas and Virginia share fossil remnants and rock strata with north-west Ireland. (Of course, it's not why bluegrass music shares so much with traditional Irish music. That is the result of 19th-century migration, though it does reinforce the idea that we are neighbouring pieces of the same jigsaw.)

As we've seen with the Aboriginal songlines, there are examples in certain indigenous cultures of memories stretching back to the birth of continents, though it's hard to tell if this Scots Gaelic poem is one of them. In all likelihood it isn't, but the *cailleach* is truly ancient. She's a remnant of the nature gods that were here long before the Celts arrived, and she represents an intuitive understanding of plate tectonics and geological time. Some of the most resonant lines from the poem are those in which she describes her diet, which is clearly that of a pre-farming hunter–gatherer. *Bu bhiadh miamh maidne dhomh, Duileasg Lioc an Eigir, Agus creamh an Sgòth* ('My wholesome morning food used to be dulse [red seaweed] from the Rock of Eigir and the wild garlic of Sgòth').

FINDING WITCHES

Although the *cailleach* predates the Irish language by a few millennia, there's a strong
connection to her when we speak Irish, because over
the two thousand years the language has existed,
it has been infused with much of her attitude and
outlook. She has managed to embed herself deeply
in the lexicon and its accompanying folklore.

A word for a particular awkward tree stump is
cailleach, and the act of scaremongering is *cailleach
an uafáis* ('the hag of terror'). The egg-case of a small

shark, dogfish or skate is known as *sparán na caillí mairbhe* ('the purse of the dead witch'), and a great sleep is referred to as *codladh na Caillí Béarra* ('the sleep of the Old Woman of Beara'), in reference to the witch's current manifestation on earth, which is a huge boulder looking out into the Atlantic at the tip of the Beara Peninsula in Co. Cork.

I make it my business to visit this stone whenever I'm there, as I feel she is still an important part of who I am today. The rock is a forlorn, craggy lump that has been badly eroded, but within it is the essence of what she once was. The 14th-century Book of Lecan claims that she was the goddess of the people of Corcu Duibne, from whom I learnt my Irish as a child. The lands of Corca Dhuibhne (as it now is) are those at the end of the Dingle Peninsula in Co. Kerry. In stories and songs I heard when growing up the *cailleach* was a common presence there, though there was no trace of her in my Dublin life.

It was the words of the Cailleach Bhéarra that I had chanted at the Loughcrew cairn, and it was believed that she had passed through many life-times, always going from old age to youth in a cyclical fashion. Her offspring became the initial settlers of Corca Dhuibhne, and their descendants were the same elderly women I used to visit when wandering the area looking for sweets, and they were also the old men sitting at the pier for whom I used to run errands.

These people not only kept her memory alive but their bony and withered bodies made them seem like apparitions of her. This was an impression intensified by the tendency of the older women to wear black knitted shawls to Mass on Sundays – shawls they'd throw over their heads in the rain. I was convinced, for example, that our next-door neighbour was a *cailleach*, and I would hide behind my grandmother's skirts if the neighbour got off her bike to speak to us.

The rock in Co. Cork presents the *cailleach* as a bereft, forsaken figure, biddably waiting through the turn of every tide for her husband, the sea god Manannán, to return and make her whole again;

but when I visit her I like to imagine her in her prime. I try to ignore the eons of *aimliú* (spoiling by exposure to weather) that has left her wizened and clad in grey lichen. I see past the tawdry trinkets and tattered rags left by other pilgrims and imagine a time when she was vital. I listen for her heartbeat, which people say can still be heard within the stone, though it is so slow now that it is in rhythm with the retreating motion of the waves.

Even on the warmest summer day the rock feels slightly damp. Some say this is because an element of her is still alive within it, at least during the months of growth and harvest when she hides here. Only at Samhain (1 November) does she retake her corporeal form to help bring on the winter by beating back the last vestiges of the verdant and whooshing in the cold. At least, that is according to the few stalwarts who believe she has power on this earth. They claim that she continues to be reinvigorated annually through the storms and snows of winter, before retreating again around Imbolc (1 February) into the rock, which once again takes on its damp chill.

The extent of her previous vitality is hard to imagine. It was said that not only has this semi-divine figure overseen the birth of landmasses, brought forth the annual destruction of winter and the rebirth of spring and created our greatest passage tombs and cairns but she also had the power to confer legitimacy on the kings of ancient Ireland. In the most famous poem attributed to her (though it was probably written by a monastic scribe in the 10th century who appreciated her role in fostering the matriarchal divine energy), she boasts:

I had chariots and horses then,
given by admiring kings.
I drank mead and wine with them.

This is another version of the lament I found myself chanting at Loughcrew. It was recorded by a different monk in a different manuscript, and translated by Anthony Weir. It too turns bitter as she recalls how all this was taken from her.

Now among old onion-skins
of withered women I drink whey,
myself a withered onion-skin.

My hands are bony now, and thin;
once they plied their loving trade
upon the bodies of great kings.

These lines are a good summary of how she is typically presented now. It is a cautionary tale about an immortal being who outlived all the tribes and races that descended from her and then finally, by agreeing to submit to the new power of Christianity, lost everything. She consented to wearing the veil and it led to her downfall. Over the course of the century after her conversion she aged and withered, descending into forlorn joylessness, where she would dwell in her old haunts and bemoan the loss of bygone pleasures.

Ultimately, the *cailleach* is a cypher for society's regrets about submitting to the control and confined parameters of Christianity. She is a representation of an innate desire to return to the days of paganism and an awareness of the loss we've suffered in culture and wisdom and in alienation from nature. But, beyond all that, the Cailleach Bhéarra is principally a reminder to women of the freedom and power they once had and of how far their status has fallen.

To have all this wonder and wisdom bound up within the shell of a single word is remarkable, but it is not exceptional in Irish. The loss of this wisdom shows just how challenging it is to keep the multi-dimensional vitality of old languages alive.

HOW TO RECOGNISE
THE CAILLEACH

A ll life is, of course, gloopy and dense with layers and levels of experience and insight. We tend to tune them out to help make more sense of things, but if we allow ourselves to be open, the invisible can become visible. The multidimensional weave of reality begins to reveal itself, maybe imperceptibly at first, but over time it deepens and enriches. It's what our mythology keeps stressing and it's particularly apparent when you immerse yourself in old languages.

Any word can lead you deeper into the lexicon, stumbling on snippets and shards of folk memory and experience that have been collated over millennia. Maybe they have mutated a little, but they can still be recognised, if we know how to look. Eventually, it will lead you right back to where you are now but with a deeper sense of how we are all connected, of how everything is one.

I'm keen to move on from the *cailleach* but there are just a few more loose threads that ought to be tied up first. Words like these have so many nuances and inferences that they're practically endless. Delineating and segregating them, as is done in modern dictionaries, is almost impossible.

First off, I should mention that not only did I believe that my neighbour in West Kerry looked like a *cailleach* but once a year I actually met the *cailleach* herself on the streets of Dingle, where she played a key part in the festival of Lá an Dreolín ('Wren Day') held on St Stephen's Day,

26 December. A man would dress up as an old woman and be accompanied by a gang of musicians and totemic figures, known as 'wren boys', dressed in rags, twigs, straw, moss and leaves. They would dance and play music through the streets all afternoon and then party at night.

This tradition is being revived in certain parts of Ireland and each group of wren boys will have a *cailleach* figure among them. She is often played by a man dressed in many layers of old clothes and she will have a bedraggled rope or belt around her waist, long dirty hair, a staff or broom for support and an unmistakable potency to her that is beyond human.

The following description from Scotland, from Alexander Campbell's 'Account of the Dances of the Gael, or Highlanders' (1804), is still apt. The sole performer portraying the *cailleach*

> is dressed in a very grotesque stile, having a huge bunch of keys hanging by her apron-string, and a staff to support her; for she affects to be very stiff, and lame of one

leg. When the tune strikes up, she appears hardly able to hobble on the floor; by degrees, however, she gets on a bit, and as she begins to warm, she feels new animation, and capers away at a great rate, striking her pockets, and making her keys rattle; then affecting great importance as keeper of the good things of the store-room, *ambry* [small recess in a wall], and dairy. Meanwhile some of the company present join the person who plays the tune, and sing words suitable to the character the dancer assumes – generally some nonsense of a comic cast, with which the matron, or *Cailleach*, seems wonderfully delighted.

I have yet to see a *cailleach* carrying large keys, but the description is intriguing, as it hints at an Orion-like figure – a belted warrior with items dangling from her belt and a staff raised aloft. This image is appropriate because Orion is a central mythological character of winter. It is interesting that Campbell mentions her connection to the store room and ambry, which is a storage recess for important items. It reminds us that the word *cailleach* also refers to a small alcove for storing *giúirléidí* ('knick-knacks') or to the recess in a wall for a bed.

We also have a good description of her from the tale 'Togail Bruidne Da Derga', preserved in Lebor na hUidre, the oldest extant manuscript entirely in Irish, dating from the 12th century, though the tale is clearly pre-Christian. You'll remember that Conaire Mór, the high king of Ireland, was forced to break his *geis* ('taboo') by the arrival of an old woman to the door of a warrior fort at night and demanding to be let in. The description of her (again, as translated by Whitley Stokes) makes clear that she is a *cailleach*.

> As long as a weaver's beam was each of her two shins, and they were as dark as the back of a stag-beetle. A greyish, wooly mantle she wore. Her lower hair used to reach as far as her knee. Her lips were on one side of her

head. She came and put one of her shoulders against the door-post of the house, casting the evil eye on the king and the youths who surrounded him in the hostel.

When Conaire asks her name she launches into a litany to show how multidimensional she is. Among the names she lists are

Samon, Sinand, Seisclend, Sodb, Caill ...
Níth, Némain, Nóennen, Badb, Blosc, Bloár,
Huae, óe Aife la Sruth.

Badb (Modern Irish *badhbh*) means 'hooded crow', something she is often portrayed as. In another myth, 'Togail Bruidne Dá Choca', she again appears as a crow, being described as a 'red woman' washing blood from a chariot at the crossing point of a river. By this stage Conaire is dead and his son Cormac is angling to replace him. Cormac and his men encounter her by the riverside near Athlone, and as they unyoke their chariots they notice a red woman on the edge of the ford, washing her chariot and its cushions and its harness. When she lowered her hand, the bed of the river became red with gore and with blood. But when she raised her hand over the river's edge, not a drop therein but she lifted it high; so that they went dryfoot over the bed of the river.'

When someone asked her what she was doing she stood on one foot again (adopting the pose of magical incantation, as she did in 'Togail Bruidne Da Derga'), and with one eye closed she uttered the grim prophecy that she was washing the harness of a dead king – that of Cormac himself. That communities throughout Ireland are feeling an impetus to revive the *cailleach* as part of an ancient festival is remarkable, and it's even more remarkable to encounter her in a Gaeltacht area like West Kerry, where she is part of an unbroken ritual stretching back through time.

Spending a day in Dingle immersed in Irish on Lá an Dreoilín is to come to an awareness of how our culture has always accepted life as a continuous oscillation between the tangible living existence and a spiritual state that is constantly awaiting rebirth in the next cycle. The *cailleach*, as the perfect intermediary, with a foot in both worlds, is the ideal figure to help us appreciate this dichotomy.

It is strangely pleasing that this woman, who was demonised by the patriarchy, is still part of the language I speak today. That she now exists in physical form in an increasing number of communities throughout the country once a year, and that she can be visited for the rest of the time at a shoreline rock in West Cork on the continually shifting margin between land and ocean, is something to be treasured and savoured.

SEX IN IRISH

After three chapters focused on the feminine, let us turn to the penis. Perhaps the greatest difference between the Irish spoken in the Gaeltacht and that spoken in cities and towns beyond the Gaeltacht is the chasteness of the latter. Generations of schoolchildren have searched for rude words in Irish dictionaries, only to be disappointed. To a learner it's as if the penis or vagina never existed for Irish-speakers and there appeared to be no terms for the fun that could be had with them.

Yet it should be clear by now that Irish is a gritty, earthy language, as rooted in nature as it is in esoteric realms. Certainly, matters of reproduction and the pleasures of the body are a central concern. It's unfortunate that dictionary editors and teachers over the past two centuries have been too prudish to list them. Local people tend to avoid using them around outsiders, as these *Lá Breá's* 'blow-ins' tend not to understand them, and explaining them can cause offence.

The poet Nuala Ní Dhomhnaill was brought up in West Kerry from the age of six, and she has said that she never heard words for sex until after she married, whereupon she was welcomed into the women's realm of the back kitchen and discovered an entirely new vocabulary.

I have not been inducted into this realm myself, so I must rely on one of the only published records: a short book by a young Dubliner, Dáithí Ó Luineacháin, published in the 1990s. He spent a few summers gathering words from two or three middle-aged men in West Kerry and then added to these by burrowing through old books and manuscripts. He amassed an extensive collection but, as he acknowledges in his introduction, it's only a cursory offering. There are many more words yet to be gathered. Sadly, he died soon after, and no one has yet sought to finish his work.

For topics other than sex much of the richness of the Irish lexicon was recorded by a scattering of linguists, folklorists and antiquarians who came word-gathering from all across Europe throughout the 19th century. They fanned out into the remotest western outposts to study the vestiges of what they realised was an ancient and dying culture. Each had their own agenda and ideas about the language and thus were seeking different things, but they dutifully recorded any words that seemed unusual or interesting. Regrettably, this almost never included anything that was indelicate or puerile. They simply overlooked these. They also overlooked, or were oblivious of, words and expressions concerning the private lives of women and their sexual concerns.

Some of the most renowned female *seanchaithe* ('storytellers') were known for their bawdy humour and they shared this openly with folklorists who sought their knowledge in the 1920s, 30s and 40s. However, when speaking into the wax cylinder recorder they tended to be more circumspect, censoring certain things.

Nonetheless, their true selves emerged when telling stories in the more relaxed setting of the *súgán* ('straw rope') chair by the fireside. These tales would be transcribed, but invariably the bawdier elements would be removed and the language sanitised. And so, still today, those of us who are not women living in the Gaeltacht have no access to this lexicon, and the younger generation of women in the Gaeltacht might not be getting to hear them either.

The nuanced forms of censorship at the time are hard to underestimate. Firstly, men seeking this information in the 19th century often weren't aware of what the right questions to ask women were. Secondly, if a priest was present, or if a woman thought that the priest or unknown figures might read her words, she would inevitably censor herself. Either way, our knowledge of sexuality in Irish is patchy and skewed towards the male viewpoint.

Ó Luineacháin in his dictionary relied principally on the knowledge of the three older men in the West Kerry Gaeltacht and on the few works of literature that liberally address sexual matters. These are the wildly licentious and bawdy 18th-century comic poem 'Cúirt an Mheán Oíche' ('The Midnight Court') by Brian Merriman and modern novels, poems, memoirs and short stories by the likes of Pádraic Breathnach, Liam Ó Muirthile and Breandán Ó hEithir.

The greatest Irish lexicographer, and the compiler of the dictionary from which many of the words in these pages have been extracted, is an tAthair Pádraig Ó Duinnín (Father Patrick Dinneen), a Jesuit priest who often went to great lengths to avoid defining a sensitive word in an insensitive or uncouth way. His definition of *drúth* ('prostitute') includes a quotation from a law tract:

'a foolish girl ... though not wholly incapable of being useful'.

He defines *feis*, which means sexual intercourse or a feast or carnival, as 'passing the night, cohabitation, wedlock'. His predecessor Bishop John O'Brien, in his *Focalóir Gaoidhilge-Sax-Bhéarla* (1768), had taken a more moralistic stance, defining *drúth* as 'a harlot or other unchaste person' and *feis* as 'carnal communication' or 'an entertainment'.

Finding a sensitive, female-centric view of sexuality in older Irish texts is just not possible. Even in modern Irish literature all we have are the works of a few pioneering women poets who have been gradually and sporadically developing a new voice since the late 1960s. Otherwise, we are left with Ó Luineacháin's dictionary, *Ó Ghlíomáil go Giniúint: Foclóir na Collaíochta*, which offers valuable glimpses of how sex in Irish was dealt with in a less prudish and more honourable way than in other cultures.

For example, menstrual blood was *bláthscaoileadh* ('bloom release') or *bláthdhortadh* ('bloom shedding'). *An t-ádh dearg* ('the red luck') was also used, as was *tá brúdáin orm* ('I'm being crushed').

But, as I said, these terms would have been given to Ó Luineacháin by men, and many of them have a demeaning tone: *gabhaltsruth* ('groin stream'), *galar na ceirte* ('the rag sickness'), *banfhlosca* ('woman's torrent'), *bandortadh* ('woman's spilling').

The words for vagina listed in Ó Luineacháin's book are also somewhat disparaging, and they are five-fold less numerous than the words for penis. The principal words are *pis*, *pit*, *gabhal mná* and *bléin mná*, the latter two meaning 'women's groin' and 'women's crotch'. There are likely to be many wonderfully metaphorical terms that neither I nor Ó Luineacháin know about. The ones I have heard are *mong* (a thick growth of hair, a swamp or a morass), *riasc rúnda* ('hidden swamp'), *gairdín dorcha* ('dark garden'), *séanas* ('chasm', 'harelip') and *bóta* or *móta* (a mound, often of heavy clay, found in low-lying rivers and favoured by tinsmiths for use in a tempering furnace).

There are other, less pleasant terms like *gráta* ('grate'), *clais* ('gully', 'trench'), *similéar* ('chimney') and *cáilín báire* ('girl's goal'). A clitoris is a *brille*, which also means an awkward person, or a *breall* ('ugly protuberance', 'blubber lip', the knob at the end of one arm of a flail, the tip of the penis). The phrase *brille bhrealla* means 'vulgar gossip', but it could also mean the 'clitoris's clitoris' .

Ó Luineacháin's words for sexual intercourse suggest a male-dominated act of impaling or possessing. There's *slataíocht* ('stick-work'), *bodaíocht* ('pricking'), *cláraigh* (flattening against a board), *buail* ('beating'), *proiteáil* and *práisáil* (pressing or foisting on), *brúigh* ('pushing'), *bualadh craicinn* and *bualadh leathair* ('slapping skin' and 'slapping leather'), *stialláil* (cutting into strips) and *gabháil* ('capturing' or 'harnessing').

Among the less violent words are *cnagadh* ('knocking'), *fáisc* ('squeezing'), *feamáil* ('gadding'), *gioltaíocht* or *giollacht* ('attending to'), *clíth* (copulation of humans or swine) and *feis*, which was alluded to earlier and has pleasant connotations of being both sex and a celebration. There are also more standard words like *comhriachtain* ('coitus'), *céileachas* ('copulation' or 'companionship') and *gnéas* ('sex').

The two principal West Kerrymen whom Ó Luineacháin consulted gave him a rich array of words for 'penis'. There are more than fifty listed, from well-known ones such as *bod* ('penis'), *ball fearga* ('male member') and *pilibín* ('penis', 'lapwing' or 'barnacle' or a thatching tool used for drawing the straw together) to other more jokey or demeaning terms such as *cuiteog* ('earthworm') *diúilicín/diúlaman/dúlamán* (tiny shell, small suckable thing, channelled wrack), *sceidín* (a small speck, driblet), *scibirlín* (limp, hanging thing), *eireaball tosaigh* ('front tail'), *scoithín* (little whisp of flax, hair or hemp), *scothach* (tufted seaweed, a fence made of tree loppings), *éinín* ('little bird'), *sliastánach* (strips of wood to protect oars in a rowlock, person with a shambling gait), *slibire* (pliant, dangling rod), *sleabhac* (wilted thing, draped nori seaweed) and *tuiteam/titimeán* ('dropper').

Then there are also more descriptive terms like *bliúcán* ('wild carrot'), *feirc* (hilt of a dagger, peak of a hat, a protuberance), *scadán* ('herring', 'thin man'), *meacan* ('tuberous root'), *smachtín* ('cudgel', 'bludgeon'), *cleith* ('upright rod'), *bachall* ('shepherd's staff'), *iall* ('thong', 'bootlace'), *dúid* ('pipe', the craning of the neck to one side, a cad) and *ga* ('spear').

There are also straightforward ones like *féith* ('sinew', 'muscle'), *bata* ('stick'), *geineadán* ('germinating tool'), *pionna* ('pin', 'peg'), *réad* ('thing', 'star'), *staic* ('stake', 'post'), *meamar* ('limb', 'member'), *sconnaire* ('tap'), *sáiteán* (a thruster, a stake, a young shoot), *gléas* (a tool, a flaccid or erect penis) and *tairne* ('nail').

Finally, there are a few random metaphorical words: *earc luachra* ('lizard'), *péacallach* (having a long tail), *gimidiúit* (based on *gimide*, 'coccyx'), *scáthachán* (sheltered parts of the body), *bléin* ('groin'), *an fear bán* ('the white man'), *biach* (defined in Dinneen's and O'Brien's dictionaries as *virilia viri* and *membrum virile*).

I could continue with more words to refer, in particular, to an erect penis, but that's enough to be getting on with. There are just three more words from Ó Luineacháin's collection that I want to share. The first is *cosán an ghiorria* ('cleavage', literally 'the hare's path'). Then there's *súpláil*, sucking a nipple for pleasure, and *súraic na gcluas agus na gciníos*, sucking ears and breasts. All of these are key elements of 'getting it on', which in Irish is *cuimleáil* ('rubbing'), *géageáil* ('clinching'), *glíumáil* ('groping'), *giolamas* ('fondling'), *méirínteach* ('fingering'), *peataíocht* ('petting'), *moltáil* ('flirting') or *radaireacht* ('courting').

But for a full immersion in the sensuality and sexuality of the Irish language, find a translation of 'Cúirt an Mheán Oíche' ('The Midnight Court'). Its gutsy bawdiness and black humour are immediately evident throughout its one thousand lines, which recount the story of a man being put on trial by the women in his life. With some truly filthy wordplay, raunchy imagery and not a hint of prudishness, the poem careers along helter-skelter towards a type of bondage fantasy. It lampoons Irishmen for their sexual awkwardness and inexperience while pleading for suitable stimulation and satisfaction for the sex-starved women of Ireland.

For a taste of its boisterous audacity, I've translated lines 708 to 713, which describe the futile efforts of a woman trying to arouse her impotent older lover.

Béal ar bhéal is ag
méaraíocht síos air.
Is minic do chuir sí cos
taobh anonn de,
Is chuimil a bruis ó
chrios go glún de;
Do sciobadh an phluid is
an chuilt dá ghúnga
Ag spriongar is ag sult
le moirt gan subhachas.
Níor chabhair di coigilt
ná cuimilt ná fáscadh,
Fogha da hingin, dá
huillinn, dá sála.

Mouth to mouth, and
fingering him down there.
She'd often throw her
leg right around him,
And rub her brush from
his waist to his knee;
She'd pull the blanket
and quilt from his bones,
Toying and caressing with
this husk without verve.
But tickling, rubbing
or fondling didn't help,
nor stroking her nail
on his elbows or soles.

SEAWEED

That three different seaweeds can be used as demeaning references to the penis – *scothach* ('tufted seaweed'), *sleabhac* ('nori', 'laver', 'sloke') and *dúlamán* ('channelled wrack') – seems unfair to these super-nutritious vegetables of the ocean. Especially to *sleabhac*, which is one of the most nutritious and life-giving plants in Ireland, with ten times more calcium than milk and an array of minerals, including copper, iron, magnesium, manganese, phosphorus, potassium, selenium and zinc, as well as vitamins A, B, C, D, E and K.

Along with other kinds of *feamainn* (seaweeds and sea vegetables), *sleabhac* thrives in the cold Irish waters, and they all combined to form a vital component in Irish society, providing food, fertiliser and fuel. In winter, when the land goes to sleep and no longer offers its bounty of fruit, nuts, cereals and vegetables, *sleabhac* and other seaweeds are at their most abundant, and so it should be no surprise that they found an important place in the language too.

The word *sleabhac* seems to contain the knowledge people had of its potency – that it was rich in folic acid and several alkaloids with antioxidant properties, together with chlorophyll, a natural detoxifier. For the word can also refer to the resilient mix of tough dermal bone and keratinised cells that form the inside of an animal horn – the part that gives a horn its strength.

Certainly the notion of associating the attribute of solidity with *sleabhac* doesn't come from its appearance, which even at its best, in full winter prime, is that of decomposing vegetable sludge. Its ragged, clingfilm-like membranes are only one or two cells thick and can be purple, pink, grey or black. They look their finest underwater but even then they are still most like wan, slender stretches of frayed silk that drape themselves over rocks when the tide goes out.

It is this characteristic that gives *sleabhac* its second meaning: to droop, slouch, fade, flag or become limp. *Tá an bláth ag sleabhcadh* means 'The flower is wilting', and *ag sleabhcadh leis an ocras* means 'limp from hunger'. Look for the droopiest plant on the shore and you'll have found *sleabhac*. If it happens to be a rich supply, make a note of where it is, as you now have access to a vitamin and nutritional larder that will power you through many winters to come.

A mystery is why the words *sleabhac* and *feamainn* are also used to refer to the Devil, and they are often employed in curses. *Go dtuga an sleabhac leis é* means 'May the devil take him'. A demon is also replaced by the word 'seaweed' in the phrase *Bíodh an fheamainn aige*, meaning 'Let him go to the devil,' or 'He can go to blazes,' although it literally means 'Let him have the seaweed.'

If I were to put *mo mhaide san fheamainn* (offer my tuppence-worth, literally put 'my oar into the seaweed'), I'd say that it arises from the very fact that it was so highly esteemed. The factiousness that broke out over seaweed rights among coastal families is legendary, with every family zealously guarding its own carefully delineated supply. Just as with turf-cutting today, there were constant tensions between neighbours who felt that someone else may have encroached on their patch. So, it is possible that seaweed became a curse word to fling at the accused. This interpretation is borne out by the proverb *Tá mise ceart, bíodh an fheamainn ag an bhfear eile* ('I'm okay, let the man have the seaweed'). The antagonism over turf-gathering in summer saw its equal in the practice of seaweed-gathering in winter.

That seaweed-gathering was primarily a winter practice is well attested to in the Irish name of the most common and useful of Irish kelps, *Laminaria hyperborea*, which is *feamainn gheimhridh* ('winter seaweed'). Once the winter storms strike, this seaweed tumbles ashore in abundant jumbles of brownish-red clumps with sea rods attached. It was regarded as an offering from the sea to be spread on the dormant land to nourish the soil for the season ahead.

On bleak December mornings when a swell was spotted, men, women and children would rush to the shore to gather the *feamainn gheimhridh* before the undertow of the ebbing tide covered it with sand and ruined it. It was no easy task, wading out to their necks in the freezing waters to haul in this bounty, followed by long hours spent cutting the rods off each plant so that they could be burnt separately for kelp-powder making.

Winter seaweed traditions are still alive in many parts of Ireland. On Tory Island *dúlamán* ('channelled wrack') is considered at its best at Christmas, when the tips are cut to around thumb-length and boiled to make 'the healthiest food imaginable', as one man told the folklorist Seán Ó hEochaidh in the 1950s. An ancient poem claims that the *dúlamán* from Carraig Chormadáin, near Glencolumbkille, Co. Donegal, was one of the two foods that St Colm Cille survived on – the other being green clover from na Dumhcha.

The esteem in which *dúlamán* was held (that is, the version of the word meaning 'seaweed', not 'shrivelled penis') can be seen in the love song 'Dúlamán', made famous again by Clannad on their 1976 album of the same name, featuring Enya. A different melody for the song was recorded by Altan in 1993. The first line of the song is *Dúlamán na binne buí, dúlamán Gaelach* ('Bladder wrack of the yellow cliff, Irish bladder wrack'), used in reference to a woman considered as beautiful as this common brown algae with paired bladders on each side of a prominent midrib and with weakly spiralled drooping fronds that have male and female reproductive receptacles in a swollen area at the tips of its fronds. It's certainly different from equating one's beloved with a red, red rose or a pure while lily.

Other interpretations claim that the song is about a seller of a type of seaweed used to dye cloth who is conversing with a seller of edible seaweed who wishes to marry the first seaweed-seller's daughter. Or it's about Ireland and Ulster, personified by different seaweeds, discussing the starvation conditions in Ulster during a famine period in the 17th century. One part refers to *Bróga breaca dubha ar an dúlamán gaelach | Tá bairéad agus triús ar an dúlamán gaelach* ('The Irish seaweed has speckled black shoes | The Irish seaweed has a cap and trousers').

The popularity and longevity of the song, thought to be at least a century old, possibly three, suggests that people enjoyed being compared to seaweed – presumably in terms of its vibrancy and nutritiousness, as opposed to its appearance.

Duileasc ('dulse') is another seaweed that thrives in winter, when its flavour matures. It too has elements of mythology built up around it. Tory Islanders refer to three types of it: *duileasc ropáin*, *creathnach* and *duileasc buan*. The first was best picked before St Patrick's Day, the second preferably in May, and *duileasc buan* ('everlasting dulse') could be picked any time between May and August. Micí Whiting, a fisherman from Inis Bó Finne in Donegal, says the difference is that small mussels grow on the *creathnach*, while *duileasc* has none.

There are no English words differentiating these seaweeds: they are all simply known as 'dulse', which is an anglicized form of the Irish word. Presumably some English-speakers noticed that a smaller, sweeter dulse (*creathnach*) grows on the backs of mussels, but it appears as though no one ever bothered to name it.

All three are sweeter and stronger when growing in the most exposed and coldest waters, as a rougher current makes for better flavour. In West Kerry dulse is known as *míobhán*, which elsewhere means a stimulating sea breeze or a form of intoxication, both of which are apt metaphors for the jolt you get from a mouthful of delicious, mineral-rich *duileasc*. Bean Uí Bhuirtínig, who was in the poorhouse in Killarney in 1938, recalled collecting *míobhán* after spring tides in her youth in Cahersiveen and drying it on the flagstones of the shore; some of it was fed to children as a nutritional booster, while the rest was sold for five shillings per half bag.

With the revival of interest in seaweed in recent years, perhaps some of these seaweed words will survive. Among them are *casfheamainn* ('spiral wrack'), *míoránach* ('serrated wrack'), *coirleach* ('oarweed'), *ríseach*, *réamóga* or *ruánach* (all meaning 'thongweed'), *rufa* ('sea-belt'), *claimhe* ('furbelows'), *líneáil ghorm* ('green alga'), *ruálach* ('sea-laces'), *samaide* ('edible sea moss') and *eireaball cait* ('horsetail kelp').

But these are just a smattering of the dozens of types of seaweed that coastal communities once had names for, and there were many variations of each one. *Copóg* was similar to *coirleach* except that it was wider and not as long or curled at the top. *Duilleacha* was a similar variety, which when added to *feamainn bhuí* ('knotted wrack') or *boilgín* (another word for 'bladder wrack') in spring as fertiliser had to be first exposed and let fade before the sods were turned.

Sraoilleach was a form of seaweed very like *coirleach*, though flimsier, veined and slightly indented, making it unsuitable for kelp-making. *Scothach* ('mayweed') equalled *coirleach* and *copóg* in its ability to add strength, vigour and weight to the kelp (and it had the advantage of emitting iodine if burnt with *coirleach* and *slat mara*, 'sea rod'). *Eireaball cait* had a related form called *gruaig na caillí mara* ('hair of sea witch'), with larger, broader fronds, which also grew in the same sheltered depths 'between the arches near small sandy holes on the weed-covered bottom', according to the Connemara man Séamas Mac an Iomaire, who in 1938 recorded his local seaweeds in the book *Cladaí Chonamara* ('The Shores of Connemara').

And, of course, there was also a separate lexicon for seaweed-gathering. There was *bacán*, a hook for harvesting rods and fronds on the Aran Islands; *cál leannógach*, the mushy green clumps of old sea plants that get washed up on the tide; *cainniúir*, and *turscar*, which as we saw earlier means 'spam' but can also mean washed-up rotten seaweed. Micí

Whiting lists *sláthach* in his collection of words and phrases, *Seanchas agus Nathanna Cainte Mhicí Whiting*, as the word for seaweed that rots under a layer of sand, which one only discovers by putting one's foot through it. He writes that *cannabhaire* refers to a man in charge of loading and strapping down seaweed onto a horse or ox while women were collecting it. One of my favourite words, though, is *roc*, which refers to wrinkles in general but specifically to the gentle puckering on the water's surface caused by seaweed tips brushing it from below.

Perhaps the current interest in seaweed for cooking and cosmetics may stimulate a *roc* in the minds of people to return to these words.

DIVINE INSPIRATION

The Irish word for 'inspiration' is *inspioráid*, which is hardly inspiring. It is functional and easy to remember, but it doesn't sound like Irish, and would be rarely used in the Gaeltacht. People there would approach the idea from a different angle. They might reach for the word *gríosadh*, which refers to being excited or sparked by something, as *gríos* means 'hot embers'. (It can also mean to blush, or something glowing or smouldering, so as a verb it can be used for both toasting bread and inspiring the soul.) Or they could choose *spreag*, which means to incite or arouse, although two generations ago it meant 'rebuke' or 'admonish'.

Old Irish has a far more compelling word, which goes beyond anything *inspioráid* can summon. It has the nuances you'd expect from a culture that was immersed in taking direction from, and communicating with, the natural and spirit worlds. That word is *imbas* (Modern Irish *iomas*). It derives either from *im-fiuss* (with *fiuss* being an early form of the Modern Irish *feas*, meaning 'knowledge', thus 'into knowledge') or from *im-bas*, which means 'into the palms of your hands', with *bos* being the modern word for 'palms', as in *bualadh bos*, which means 'applause', and *bulla bó báisín*, which refers to how cows stroll back satiated from the milking-parlour in a wandering and dispersed manner, as opposed to a *streoillín* ('stripleen'), which is how cows approach a milking-parlour, in a purposeful ordered line. This word can also mean the Pleiades, but that's another matter.

The palms of your hands are not the first thing you think of when considering inspiration, but it makes more sense when you know that *imbas* was most commonly used in the phrase *imbas forosnai*, with *forosnai* meaning 'that which illuminates'. So the idea is inspiration that illuminates, and it refers specifically to the act of looking into the future and chanting or reciting prophecy in the form of poetry. Often this practice involved the use of sensory deprivation in order to pass into a trance-like state. Terms like these are perhaps too intense for our pragmatic world, which is why they fell out of use; but I still haven't explained the reference to the palm of the hand.

For that we need to turn to a 10th-century glossary written by a bishop and king of Munster who was beheaded in AD 908. His bleeding skull was given to the King of Mide, who kissed it, saying, 'It was an evil deed to cut off the holy bishop's head; I shall honour it, and not crush it,' while he paraded it around his fort three times as a mark of respect.

The beheaded bishop was Cormac mac Cuileannáin, and he gave a full account of *imbas forosnai* in his glossary Sanas Cormaic ('Cormac's Narrative'), which describes it as a means for a poet to access inspiration by first chewing the raw flesh of a pig, dog or cat and then placing it on a flagstone behind a door. That's the first part of the ritual, after which the poet then chants an incantation to his 'idol gods' for a day or two and places his palms over his face and eyes to enter a trance state, which lasts for a *nómad* – meaning either three days and nights or nine days – from the proto-Celtic *naumetos*, meaning a ninth. (Nowadays a *nómad*, spelled *nóiméad*, means a 'minute', but that's presumably because the old word got mixed up with the new term *nóimeint*, or *neomat*, which was a gaelicisation of 'moment'.)

In his description Cormac suggests this shamanic process was intense and emphasises the importance of having a facilitator on hand to protect initiates from doing harm to themselves or others or from being yanked out of a trance at a particularly inopportune moment. His was an early version of the buddy system that some people adopt when taking LSD or mushrooms, with someone on hand to look out for their partner in case of a bad trip.

This idea of placing the palms over the face is also used in the alternative therapy Reiki to enhance the power of the Third Eye when receiving divine knowledge and visions. And the practice of accessing wisdom by imbibing something and then entering a state of sensory deprivation in a darkened room (while uttering incantations) is common to many cultures. The initiate enters a state of heightened awareness and then the door is thrown open, or the covers are suddenly removed, and it is this sudden and instant transition from darkness to light that apparently triggers the visions.

As regards chewing the raw flesh, this is possibly an exaggeration by Cormac to denigrate the pagan practice, knowing that people loved their dogs and cats and regarded pigs as unclean. Yet the notion of eating raw meat as a way of entering another world was familiar to the Irish people, as it was a common ploy for fairies to feed you uncooked food as a means of luring you into the Otherworld – just as Eve did with her apple. In an 11th-century poem the mythological hero, Fionn mac Cumhaill, scolds a giant who is trying to get him to eat the uncooked flesh of his own horse, saying: '*beir lett, a athig, do béad, uair né dúadus biad om riam*', ('take away, O giant, your food, for I've never eaten raw food').

It's impossible to know how much truth Cormac's account contains. The terms he uses are far older than the 10th century and derive from the language of druidic learning that was meant to be understandable only to the initiated. We know from other tracts that the ritual was taught only to poet-magicians after eight years of preparatory study, so the actions of the practice should not be immediately apparent to us. Cormac, being a bishop, had no direct acquaintance with the ritual and was wary of it. He emphasises that it was against Christian teaching and was outlawed by St Patrick, who reputedly declared that 'no one who shall do that shall belong to heaven or earth, for it is a denial of baptism.'

In Irish mythology *imbas forosnai* is referred to frequently, though it was specifically a female accomplishment in the early sagas. It was only later associated with men, in particular with Fionn mac Cumhaill. He often made use of *cuill crimaind* (nuts of *imbas* or 'insight'). By swallowing one or two he could enter a zone of deep insight, and he was also able to access this state by sucking his thumb.

The best-known reference to *imbas forosnai* is in Táin Bó Cuailnge. It relates that Queen Medb was soon to march on Ulster to take the brown bull of Cooley. Her druids and sages were waiting a fortnight for an omen signalling the return of her army when a mysterious 'lone virgin of marriageable age' appeared riding on the hind pole of a chariot. Her eyes had triple irises, with delicate dark lashes that cast shadows half way down her cheeks. She explained to Medb that she was a *banfhili* ('female poet') from Connacht, and when Medb asked her if she had learnt *imbas forosnai* as part of her poetic training she said that she had. Medb then asks her to 'look' (*deca*) how the attack on Ulster will fare. The mysterious woman, Fedelm, proceeded to chant the result of her grim vision, in a lengthy litany similar to Bob Dylan's 'A Hard Rain's a Gonna Fall' – though perhaps she's closer to Joan Baez than to Dylan, with her golden hair in three tresses, two of them wound upwards on her head and the third hanging down her back, brushing her calves. She predicts a crimson bloodbath and Medb's troops being massacred by a single individual

> who will perform weapon-feats, with many a wound in his fair flesh. The hero's light is on his brow, his forehead is the meeting-place of many virtues. Seven gems of a hero are in his eyes. His spear heads are unsheathed. He wears a red mantle with clasps. His face is the fairest. He amazes womenfolk, a young lad of handsome countenance; yet in battle he shows a dragon's form … . This I know, that this army will be bloodstained from him.

She was of course referring to Cú Chulainn, he of the wild rages that sent one eyeball bulging out and the other buried so deep into his skull that a heron couldn't pluck it out.

It's a fine example of how sometimes you don't want to know what you're up against, and Medb refuses to believe it, asking the *banfháith* ('prophetess') four times for a different answer, but there's no use doubting the predictions of an *imbas forosnai*.

The details of the ritual outlined in Sanas Cormaic are not found anywhere else, but that's maybe to be expected. That a secret ritual like this was recorded even once is unusual – perhaps this was why the poor author was beheaded. Ceremonies such as these were covert, strictly for the chosen few who had put in the years of study and preparation.

The bishops and abbots, from St Patrick onwards, would all have felt threatened by anything that might empower people to access insight directly rather than through the Church. Cormac's prime motivation for including it might not have been to share it with others but to slander it by tainting it with inaccurate details.

We know that practices similar to *imbas forosnai* survived into the medieval age in Britain. An account by Gerald of Wales of a 12th-century journey around Wales describes *awenyddion*, 'inspired people' who

> when consulted upon any doubtful event roar out violently, are rendered beside themselves, and become, as it were, possessed by a spirit. They do not deliver the answer to what is required in a coherent manner; but the person who skilfully observes them will find, after many preambles ... the desired explanation conveyed in some turn of a word. They are then roused from their ecstasy, as from a deep sleep, and, as it were, by violence compelled to return to their proper senses. After having answered the questions, they do not recover until violently shaken by other people.

Cormac in his glossary identified two other practices of illumination closely linked with the *imbas forosnai*, namely *dichetal do chennaib* (a spontaneous uttering of chanted truths without preparation) and *tenm láida* ('illumination of song'). The former, he claimed, was also banished by St Patrick because, like *imbas forosnai*, it involved supernatural contact with pagan gods, whereas *tenm láida* was more to do with performing recitations in a soothing way, to relax and clear the mind, much like meditation. *Dichetal do chennaib*, on the other hand, is an altered state of consciousness accessed by chanting a repetitive song or phrase. Its purpose was to access the gods or ancestors directly and so was more threatening to Christianity.

The word *chennaib* in the plural of *cenn* (Modern Irish *ceann*, 'head' or 'forefront'). So the phrase is either 'chanting the future' or 'chanting from heads', suggestive of Hamlet accessing truth while addressing Yorick's skull. There are numerous accounts of skulls speaking truth to power in the sagas, possibly because beheadings were common even up to the 16th century, when 80 rebel skulls were impaled on the railings of Dublin Castle by Elizabethan forces.

The Ulster hero Conall Cernach claimed that he never passed the night without the head of a slain Connacht warrior on his pillow: *O ra-gabus gai im láim nach menic robá cen chend Connachtaig fóm chind oc cotlud.* The ancient phrase is comprehensible to speakers of Modern Irish, who would render it *Ó ghabh mé ga im lámh nach minic a chodail mé gan cheann Connachtach faoi mo cheann mar cheannadhairt.*

As part of Fedelm's dire prophecy to Medb she warned that the attack would result in 'a thousand severed heads', which proved true, as Cú Chulainn smote skulls in every direction until he himself was beheaded by Lugaid.

Once a head was detached it became a trophy to be mounted on a forked branch or stone or on the ramparts of a fort. The sagas also refer to them being stored by the fireside, covered with a hood – perhaps to smoke or dry them. The risk in doing this is that when the hood was removed, or accidentally fell off, it was said that the head occasionally sprang to life, spouting prophecy or criticism of those present. It's a reversal of *imbas forosnai*, whereby covering the eyes and face brings on the rush of words and ideas. Even with the brains scooped out and mixed with lime to form a solid ball-like trophy, heads were still said to come back to life. One of these brain-balls became embedded in the skull of Conchobar, King of Ulster, and then later leapt out of its own accord when the king began a deluded attack on trees. In fact people loved beheadings so much that when classical works were translated into Irish, such as Dares Phrygius' *History of the Fall of Troy*, we inserted extra beheadings, like Mexicans adding chilli to season food.

Assessing whether or not *imbas forosnai* was ever a genuine practice is to adopt a dichotomy unknown in an era of unexplained phenomena and bumps in the night, when the lines between reality and fantasy were still blurred. This was a time when a word like *aingeal* could mean both 'angel' and a burnt cinder taken from the fire and given as protection to children going out at night, or when a word like *aimsím* could mean either 'I reach for' or 'I bewitch'. This was after all a culture in which *dreag* could mean either a sling to help carry an awkward load or a star-like light that followed the course of a coffin to the graveyard or the path of a drowned body from sea to shore.

LIGHTS IN THE SKY

This notion of lights in the sky having meaning reminds me of *riastradh* ('contortion'). That Cú Chulainn's fiery warp spasms might have been passing comets prompts the question whether other celestial manifestations have influenced the language. Irish, after all, existed in a world of darkness, especially in winter, when the patina was inky grey from late afternoon to mid-morning, relieved only occasionally by burning foul-smelling lumps of sheep and cow fat or wick dipped in whale oil, or, in some northern coastal regions, with the bodies of the *gearr úisc* ('storm petrel').

We'll explore some light-themed words, but first I should mention how the *gearr úisc* could be made to produce light from its dead body. *Gearr* is short for *gearrcach* ('fledgling'); *úsc* means 'grease', 'fat' or 'animal oil'. In fact this tiny bird stores so much fat and oil in its body to cope with the many months it spends at sea that, when killed, its body can no longer keep hold of it, and oil is secreted into its digestive tract. People realised that this transformed them into ideal candles once a tarred wick was stuffed into its windpipe.

While this proved a handy source of light, it wasn't very reliable, as fishermen could catch storm petrels only before a storm, when, by rights, fishermen oughtn't to be at sea at all. It was only then that a petrel would risk approaching a boat to seek shelter on its lee side.

Landlocked communities used a different form of *úsc* for light, as that word can also mean the pith or resin emitted by trunks of Scots pine that have been buried in bogs for thousands of years. The millennia of burial concentrates the natural oils in the timber, forming a black liquid tar or petroleum that made the ancient branches ideal as torches.

Sop is another word for this. It means a torch made from bog-deal splinters, though it can also mean a wisp or handful of hay, straw or heather. For example, a *sop pice* ('wisp of heather') was used in scouring dairy vessels. I mentioned earlier that the word *sopóg* can also be used to describe a torch made of bog-deal splinters or a bundle of straw in thatching. The torches were made from long-stemmed bushes, from bunches of bog-deal slips, from tight-bound bundles of reeds, from pitchforks or from sods of turf soaked in grease and borne aloft on poles that were then carried on high to form a procession.

Certainly lights appearing mysteriously from the darkness were an evocative occurrence. The most common were will-o'-the-wisps, flashes of flame that appear on bogs when methane ignites spontaneously. *Liam na sopóige* was one term for this; another is *tine shionnaigh* or *tine an mhadra rua*, both of which mean 'fire of the fox'. I've also heard *tine ghealáin*, which means 'flash of fire' and can refer to either will-o'-the-wisps or flashes of summer lightning.

The most frequently used word for lightning is *tintreach*, and its genitive form, *tintrí*, appears in many words for fire in the sky. *Caor thintrí* means 'fireball' and 'meteor'. It can also mean 'thunderbolt', though I prefer the term *farcha tintrí* for thunderbolt, with *farcha* being the cudgel that the *cailleach* uses to beat back the summer vegetation in preparation for winter.

Saighneán is another word for flashes of lightning, as is *splanc*, although my favourite is *saighead ghealáin*, literally 'arrow of brightness'. Other terms for this are *cló tintrí*, *caoraíl*, *casair thine* and *scal tintrí*. The word for sheet lightning is *foscladh*, which comes from the verb *foscail* or *oscail* ('to open'), as though the sky were being ripped open to reveal what lies beyond.

More mysterious forms of night-time lights are *tinte chrios*, which are flashes of fire sparked on the stones of a road by a horse's hoofs, and *méarnáil*, which describes the phosphorescent light that can appear on land in certain conditions and which is different from *barraois*, which is phosphorescent light at sea. The term for the luminous track of a boat through phosphorescence in summer is *tine ghealáin*, and it can also mean the mysterious light emitted from putrid fish or rotten wood.

Maybe *tine ghealáin* would have been an apt title for this book, as what I am hoping to capture is that luminance that arises from the depths of languages – the way they shine a faint light on the past and illuminate some of our murkier memories and practices. In fact the word *siolla* ('syllable') also means a glint of sunlight, as if every word is constructed from one or more particles of light.

Moving on to larger bursts of light in the sky, we must turn to the most extensive compilation of ancient records in Ireland, the annals, which chronicle everything from dragons to famines. The best-known collection of these was compiled by a Franciscan and three laymen in the 17th century.

Their collection, the Annals of the Four Masters, contains a reference to an incident in the townland of Ros Deala, near Kilbeggan, Co. Westmeath, in AD 1054. A *cloichtheac tenedh fuirccsin isin aer* ('round tower' or 'belfry') of fire was seen hovering in the air. It remained there for five hours (or nine hours, according to a source in the 14th-century Book of Ballymote) on Sunday 23 April. While this fire rocket remained aloft above Ros Deala, witnesses claimed that *eoin dubha diairmidhe ind agus ass, agus aon en mor ina medon* ('innumerable black birds passed in and out of it, with one large bird in the middle of them'). When the smaller birds wanted to enter the steeple, they first flew in under the large bird's wings – *theigheadh na heoin bheaga foa eitbhsidhe an tan théicccdís isin cloictheach.* In Modern Irish this would be *théadh na héan bheaga faoi eití an t-éan nuair a théidís in san chlogtheach* ('the little birds would go under the wings of the bird when they went into the belfry').

There is no easy explanation for something as mysterious as this. Scholars suggest that the word 'bird' here can be regarded as a metaphor for some flying entity unknown to the observers. These entities at one point swooped down and raised up a greyhound that was in the middle of the *baile* ('settlement'). After sucking it up into the sky they let it drop, killing it. They then took up three cloaks and two shirts and let them drop in the same manner, after which the large bird pulled an oak tree out of the earth by its roots, according to the account in the Book of Ballymote.

The description sounds like a tornado or hurricane, but why the flaming belfry? It allows for the possibility that it was a spaceship with a tractor beam or suction vortex beneath it, although the fire flaming out of it doesn't make it sound like a very sophisticated one.

Either way, it's a good example of how Irish is *adhantach* ('apt to kindle'; the word also means 'thoughtful', 'lightheaded' or 'spirited'). Maybe *deargtha* is more fitting still: it means the ability to light up but also to prepare the soil for planting – or a grave for burial.

THE ILLUMINATION
OF LANGUAGE

L ight has always been regarded as a source of wisdom within the Irish language, or at least it was associated with wisdom. There was a recognition that it could spark inspiration through the arrangement of certain words, as seen in *iomas gréine* ('sun inspiration'), which refers to blisters caused by the sun on the leaves of certain herbs that, when eaten, give the gift of poetry.

And even within the fire itself there was wisdom. *Corrchogailt* refers to the green and blue figures that can be seen on the hearth when raking the fire at night. They resemble glow-worms and are said to predict the chance of frost or rain in the following days. You also find this association in the word *léas*, which means a ray of light or energy but can also mean a bright spot and a streak of reason. Some other meanings of *léas* are an incomplete rainbow, a blush, a luminance in the sky indicating bad weather, an ear of corn, a pimple and a welt.

From *léas* comes the word *léaspáin*, the dancing coloured lights that appear before your eyes at times when you drift a little too far towards other dimensions. It's like *scrimplíní*, which, you'll remember, are real or supernatural lights that dance before one's eyes. English doesn't seem to need such a word, but for Irish-speakers it was considered central enough to warrant separate words.

The Otherworld was always associated with radiance; supernatural beings shone with a peculiar lustre, as though an internal luminance arose from within. *Leaspáin* implies a recognition of this but also of the fact that everything is built of light and that, if we allow our attention to reach too far into the weft and weave of things through meditation or other rituals, we can get too close to these elements and become distorted.

The illusion we live by is that our world is composed of heavy matter, but if we dare widen our focus beyond the limited inputs provided by our senses we realise that it is far closer to being built on light, and all the interactions between things can be seen as minute flashes of illumination. A little spark here, a spark there, when two things engage. It's how electrons communicate and it's how we communicate too, which makes the fact that *siolla*, which means a syllable and a glint of light, all the more apt.

Irish seems to see light everywhere, from *méarnáil* (the phosphorescent luminance arising from the land) to *barraois* (phosphorescence at sea) and even to *tine thanaí* (a phosphorescent light seen on the teats and udders of cows in wet

weather). The illuminations of a fire were differen-
tiated too, with *brúid* being 'smouldering ashes', as
opposed to *luaith*, 'dead ashes'. These were different
from *aibhleoga* ('cinders') and *gríosacha* ('burning
embers').

Then there are the many forms of pre-dawn
light, from the initial hint of dawn, *breacadh an
lae* ('daybreak') to the gradual brightening of the
pre-dawn sky, *bánú an lae* ('the whitening of the
day') to *fáinne geal an lae* ('the first bright ring of
daylight') and, finally, *éirí na gréine* ('sunrise').

The language seems aware that there is an
unfathomable amount of lightness everywhere
in this world, even if our minds are programmed
not to focus on it but to look instead at the darker,
denser bits. It's like going to the cinema and training
one's mind to focus only on the black frame around
each brightly illuminated scene on the screen.

Certainly the world of Irish mythology is
suffused with light. Fionn mac Cumhaill, the great
hero, gets his name from *fionn* ('white', 'shining',
'sincere', 'wise'). (Or, perhaps, the name came first

and meanings like 'sincere' and 'wise', arose by association.) The word *fionn* is found in the names of many Celtic deities and heroic figures, suggesting that they were seen as emanating radiant light. Remember the earth goddess Bóinn, whose corpse created the River Boyne? Her name derived from *bó fhionn* (the white, shining or radiant cow), and you'll remember that the *vinda* in Govinda comes from the Sanskrit *uind* (to find out or know), which is related to this same early Celtic word, *vindos* ('white' or 'light'). Likewise, a famous magical salmon who brought wisdom from a well in the Otherworld to the River Shannon and to Fionn mac Cumhaill was named Fintan, meaning the white or shining one.

Lugh, the great god of skill and art (or of the sun, as some experts claim), who first recorded seeing Tonn Clíodhna and her two sister waves when he arrived from Tír na nÓg ('The Land of Youth'), has a name meaning either to shine or to swear an oath. His annual festival, Lughnasa, held at the beginning of August, gives us the Irish name for August, *Lúnasa*.

This festival is rarely held now but even forty years ago it was common for communities to gather on hilltops, light fires and play games – the ultimate game being to leap through the fire, plunging into or over the flames to emerge into the darkness on the far side. These fires were to ensure Lugh's help for a successful harvest and were always followed by even larger fires at the festival of Samhain, which marked the end of the harvest and the arrival of the *cailleach*, who brought with her the darkness of winter.

Communities would then hunker down through the dark season with whatever meagre light they had: a *brobh* (a single rush dipped in tallow used as a candle), a *trilseán* (a meagre torch of plaited rushes) or a *páideog* (a soft string of flax fibre dipped in suet; the word can also mean an untidy housekeeper or a messy eater).

The idea was to wait out the winter in the hope that light would return at Imbolc, which was the next fire festival, held on 1 February. Strips of cloth or ribbons would be placed outdoors to catch the first light of dawn or the dewdrops that would be infused with *fáinne geal an lae* ('the first bright ring of daylight'). This cloth, *Brat Bhríde*, was believed to possess curative powers that were used all year.

Does one need to know any of these light manifestations and references to speak Irish today? Probably not, but as we've seen, knowing such things – that our world was once infused with an awareness of light, that the year moved from fire festival to fire festival and that the names of these festivals, Lúnasa, Samhain and Bealtaine, are still used as the months of the year – enriches our understanding of the world.

Knowing these things also helps us appreciate our contemporary existence, which, as it happens, is now trying to grapple with the realisation that our world is less dense, more nebulous and more light-filled than ever imagined. It is built on a matrix of constantly shifting interactions on multiple planes, rather than on a solid series of things. Irish, with its malleability and bias towards ambiguity, is suited to help us contend with this new way of thinking.

Such an outlook has always been comfortable with a mutable, capricious reality that blends seamlessly with the Otherworld beneath the ground and beyond the seas. In fact it took some effort to adapt the language's tendency towards ambiguity to the more limited Newtonian outlook of delineable, material things that developed in the 17th and 18th centuries.

SPECIFICITY

That Irish has inclusiveness, uncertainty and transience encoded into it should not be taken to mean that it cannot also cope with specificity: it is just that it favours the wider angle. After all, this is a language that has a word for a reaper's handful of corn, cut with a sickle and simultaneously gathered in the left hand. It's *luchtar*, and three of them gathered together form a sheaf. (The sickle that is used to cut a *luchtar* often had a fly trapped in a tiny box strapped to its handle, as this bestowed a blessing on the blade that was believed to give it greater cutting power.)

Then there's *biorrach*, which is a marshy field but is very similar to *biorach*, a muzzle band with spikes for placing over a calf's or colt's mouth and nose to prevent it suckling on its mother, and *buicmín*, which is a piece of wood used to fasten a cord that binds the foreleg to the horns of a cow.

This aptitude for specificity that also allows for a periphery of uncertainty and mystery caters for all eventualities, just as an old oak has within it the adaptability to cope with drought and floods, plague and tempest.

Old languages with such wide parameters for coping with the real and the unreal, the sacred and profane, foster a reassuring sense that they can cope with whatever is thrown at them. This offers a root-edness, a solid existential certainty, that is hard to knock off kilter. It is the basis for the idea of the *ceap* mentioned earlier: the tree trunk hammered deep into the ground to provide a sturdy base for the anvil on which to bash away at life. It allows for a moment-by-moment acknowledgement of the essential core of all things, and it also maintains the freedom to adapt as needed.

There's a great word in Old Irish that conveys this ability to be extremely specific and also suitably vague in a single term. That word is *corrguinecht*, which describes the essential crane-ness of something, with *corr* meaning a crane, heron or stork. The word is associated with satire, divination and other supernatural acts, and it conveys a particular physical stance to adopt while performing these acts.

O'Davoren's 16th-century glossary defines *corr-guinecht* as 'being on one foot, one hand and one eye' while satirising. The tale 'Bruiden Da Choca' describes a woman uttering a prophecy while standing on one foot with one eye closed. Likewise, in 'Togail Bruidne Da Derga' ('The Destruction of Da Derga's Hostel'), you'll remember that the *cailleach* turned up at the hostel where Conaire, the High King of Ireland, was staying to get him to break his *geis*. Before she launches into a litany of her 32 names, she stands on one foot and holds her arm up high.

Whether this crane-esque quality is merely a one-footed dance or is something more profound is hard to say, but cranes were often symbols of sacredness. They were believed by druids to carry the soul from one incarnation to the next, and they were venerated in Hindu, Buddhist and Taoist philosophies. They are depicted in the Book of Kells, and one is carved into an eighth-century high cross in Co. Tipperary.

The Brehon Laws, *An Féineachas*, describe the *peata corr* ('pet crane') as being the third most popular pet after dogs and cats. In the Middle Ages they were trained to kneel or bow when a bishop gave a benediction before dinner. Apart from the role of cranes in the transmigration of the soul, their power lay in the belief that their single open eye could stare directly into the Otherworld and that, by standing on one leg, they could shift between worlds without being fully present in either.

There's a famous tale of a woman, Aífe, who was transformed into a crane by a spurned lover. Later the sea god Manannán used her skin to make a crane bag to carry his most valuable treasures, including the gems of ancient folklore. Once literacy arrived in Ireland he used this crane bag to carry the alphabet too. Thus, the crane not only carried our souls between lifetimes, but its skin was the protective casing for the most valuable elements of our heritage: first oral folklore and then the letters that became the vehicle for transporting our ancient knowledge with us from life to life down the generations.

Its reliability as a storage device was due to its holding its contents in an entirely different dimension, and they were visible on earth only at full tide. As the tide ebbed, the bag appeared to be entirely empty. This is a further example of the inter-dimensionality of the Irish world. It's similar to the *ceantar–alltar* dichotomy we encountered earlier, in which *ceantar* means 'region' or 'locality' and *alltar* means the Netherworld, with only a thin veil separating the two. Yet passage between them is possible only at certain times of the year and by certain people.

Of course when Christianity arrived it couldn't be accepted that this mysterious bird was allied to a pagan sea god, so the strong alliance with cranes was transferred to St Colm Cille, who became known as the 'crane cleric'. At the Convention of Drum Ceat, held about AD 575, he transformed a queen and her handmaiden into herons in the course of a public spat. He was defending poets from the threat of banishment by the high king Áed mac Ainmirech, who was unhappy with their *n-imad ┐ ar a ngere ┐ ar a ndoilge ┐ ar a n-aiubrethre* ('multitude, and their sourness, and their complaining, and their wicked words') – though what he actually meant was their lack of deference to him.

Some of my favourite indefinable words are those I mentioned earlier that describe fields in which something occasionally happens but in which nothing is happening now, such as *buadán*, a hillside where furze or gorse once grew but where these have been cut with a scythe or hook, leaving only stumps. (*Buadán* can also mean the quick of an animal's horn or a cloth bound around the head as a bandage.) There is also *loscán*, a patch of land from which the furze has been removed by burning rather than cutting. The primary purpose of this word is to convey the absence of the furze. It derives from *loscadh* ('to burn'), which is also used in the term *loscadh gaoithe*, a belching, blasting flatulence, bringing us back to specifics again. And since we're addressing specifics in relation to furze, we should mention *mútóg*, a glove for cutting furze, or a homemade muzzle that prevents a young calf from swallowing straw.

Such words become rivets, binding us intimately to our surroundings – often uniting two, three or more very different elements within the one term. *Storc* is a good example. It means a dwarfish pig or the corpse of one who died in an upright posture. Then there is *bladhmann*, which is either steam rising from a fermented haystack or idle boasting. A favourite, though, is *seitreach*, which is braying, whinnying or neighing in a subdued manner but also the cry of a hawk in hunting and the sound that horses make when meeting after an absence. *Seitreach* can also be used to describe the plaintive, insistent sound of a mare calling for her foal.

Old languages are rich in terms like these that emphasise our interrelatedness with all life and that reveal the empathy we have with each other and with our surroundings. They acknowledge our co-dependent relationship with nature, revealing almost as much about our inner processes and frailties as about the world around us. Yet, as we've seen, the most conspicuous words are those that hint at new ways of perceiving our reality.

QUANTUM IRISH

If we accept the validity of the *ceantar–alltar* dichotomy of this world and the Otherworld and the notion that they are always abutting each other, it affects many aspects of our understanding of life. It begins the process of paring away the overlay of conditioning that has limited our view of reality since the Newtonian outlook on physics took hold.

We're now told that there are vast invisible spaces between things and, potentially, parallel realms layered on top of each other. Reality is composed of particles, and physicists claim that there is as much space between each electron and its neutron particle as there is between a planet and the sun, proportionally. On the subatomic level, there's even more space between things.

This way of thinking seems to be allowed for in words like *scim*, *caithnín* and *crithir*, which we've already encountered. (*Scim* means a fairy film that covers the land; *cáithnín* a speck or a subatomic particle; and *crithir* the vulnerability and insubstantiality of solid objects.) Such words provide a bridge between our perceived reality and the complex network of matrices and energy fields that lie behind them. They can help weaken our conventional thought processes, which remain stubbornly embedded in their mental grooves, allowing us to perceive reality as more than the limited viewpoint that we inherited, which is invariably confined by the parameters of our conditioning.

I don't wish to overemphasise the connection between quantum thought and Irish, but it's worth noting a few similarities between it and some notions that Irish-speakers take for granted. *Toiteoir*, for example, is a noun meaning 'potato-picker' but it doesn't so much describe the picker or the potatoes as it does the act of being engaged in the interaction between the two. There are other words for 'picker' (*siolgaire, piocadóir*) and many, many words for 'potato' (*gionán, sliomach, gilín, siocaide, bodalán, creathán, clamhrán, gabhairín, cruit, gealach, angán*), but *toiteoir* homes in on the energetic exertion between both elements.

Also encompassed by the word *toiteoir* is the idea of another human digging the potatoes. That person is somewhere just ahead of the picker, just as in the atom the electron is always lingering somewhere near the proton and neutron. They are bonded by mutual dependence.

It's part of a tendency in Irish to develop words that convey the energy between different elements rather than describe a particular person, thing or action. *Tointe* is a good example. It refers to a thread that is passing between the fingers in spinning. It is different from the word for a thread, which is *snáth.* The act of being spun by a human changes it to such an extent that a new term is needed.

This happens to chime perfectly with the latest understanding of physics, which is that reality is composed of a choreography of energetic charges rather than dependable, measurable atoms moving along predictable paths. In fact electrons, atoms and molecules exist only when they're interacting with something else. All we can really know about anything is how things interact with one another, and that can never give us the full picture. There is something mysterious about it, something slippery. We've been able to create computers that rely on the interactions that form the basis of quantum mechanics without fully understanding the process.

The word *ladhar* is a further example of this. It refers to the fingers of one hand when they are all working together, gripping something or engaging collectively, as opposed to an inactive finger, which is *méar*. *Ladhar* also means a portion of land between two rivers that meet obliquely, or the space between toes. The feeling we experience when our fingers are numb with cold but are being warmed by the fire is *fualthan*.

It may seem like a moot point but if we focus on the interactions between any elements, rather than on the elements themselves, we change our perspective on the world and begin to realise that we're subservient to the energy dynamics between us. Just as a particle exists only when it hits something else, we depend for our existence on others, from conception to birth and right through life.

The verb meaning 'to work' is *obair*, but to work with reluctance or difficulty is *strácáil*. To work in a trifling manner is *priocaireacht*, and to work with overexertion is *splíontaíocht*. These convey the quality of the interaction rather than the thing that's being done or the person or thing doing it.

It brings home to us that we are multitangential arrays of interactions engaging with the world around us and each other and that we are best defined by the energy with which we relate to these things. All life on earth is composed of sets of processes – cycles of sense perception, cognition, rejuvenation, digestion and atrophy. I find it useful that Irish seeks to subtly steer me back to this truth.

WINDS

L et's return to the fiery steeple that appeared in the sky above Ros Deala in AD 1054 to explore why, if it was simply a storm, it was not referred to as a *síon, spéirling, eachan, dárdál, gailfean, confadh, garbhuaic* or any of the other words for strong storms. Maybe it was an *anfa* (a tempest or a disturbance in the elements) with *aibhleacha* in it, which are flying sparks of fire or thunderbolts with the power to split trees and ignite them.

When considering fairies earlier, we saw that winds are often regarded as the work of other-worldly beings – either actively, out of mischief, or inadvertently, as a consequence of their rushing by. This belief exists today to a certain extent. Only last year I dropped some envelopes on the way into the Baile na nGall post office (just a few weeks before it closed for ever) and a woman said to me, *Tá an buíon sí ag séideadh inniu* ('The fairy horde are blowing today').

Whirlwinds in particular were considered to be from the other realm, and the modern term for them is still *sí gaoithe*, a fairy wind, or else *séideán sí*, a fairy gust. These meanings, though, stem from a confusion that arose from there being a separate word *sí*, meaning 'gale'. Seeing cut straw in a field being lifted from the ground, or a sudden dance of leaves on an otherwise calm day, is still unsettling for us today, not to mention the unpredictable way in which a storm will pass through a yard, ignoring everything except for one girder or door, which it hurtles through the air.

One of the old women I used to visit when I was young would refer to wind that came moaning down hard from the Arctic north as *gaoth dubh* ('black wind'). It could bring illness and misfortune and it needed to be avoided as actively as you would the wind from a graveyard. The latter caution was logical, as contaminated microbes from a newly interred body could blow downwind, but the term arose from an old belief in the colours of winds.

The 10th-century Saltair na Rann ('Psalter of Quatrains') lists the colours of wind from each direction. The darkest blew in from the north and was either pitch black or void of all colour. From there, going clockwise through the cardinal and ordinal points, it goes from speckled to dark for the north-easterlies and purple for a direct east wind. The south-easterlies are regarded as yellow and red, veering towards white as you reach the straight south wind. There was green and greyish-green for the south-westerlies, and a west wind was dun-coloured. From there, dark brown and grey were for the north-westerlies.

The description is spread over a few quatrains in Eleanor Hull's translation of Saltair na Rann, which lists the cardinal points as follows:

Anair incorcra glanbda,	From the east, the smiling purple;
andess ingel gle, amra,	from the south, the pure white, wondrous;
atuaid indub gailbech, grach,	from the north, the black blustering moaning wind;
aniar' indodur engach.	from the west, the babbling dun breeze.

It's as much a chromatic map of the illumination of aspects of the cosmos as a wind chart. *Corcra* ('crimson' or 'purple') signifies the dawn in the east, as opposed to the ebbing light of evening in the west, which is given a dun colour. That northern black wind is as full of all the connotations that *dubh* ('black') has today: tempestuous, rough, dark. It summons up the frigid, stormy terrain to the north, whereas the white of the southern wind represents the light and warmth that come from the equator. It conveys that it is from this direction that the rebirth of spring spreads, together with the gradually warming land and seas, and with insects and flocks of migrating birds.

The vast majority of Ireland's wind comes from the south-west, which is where the Otherworld was most often situated. (The mystical island of Í Bhreasail was somewhere off the west coast. As we've heard, Donn, the old Irish god of the dead, lived on an island far off the Beara Peninsula in west Co. Cork, when he wasn't resident in his westerly sand dunes in Lehinch, Co. Clare.)

It's no wonder that this wind is given the most potent colour, *glas*, which means both 'green' and 'greyish blue'. *Glas* is used to describe the infinitely varied colours found on land and sea. It has been translated as 'the colour of the sky reflected in water', which is evocative, though it doesn't capture the full range of *glas*, which shifts according to what is being described.

Grass that is *glas* is verdant and flourishing, but when *glas* is used for a horse, stone or piece of tweed it refers to a plain grey or a bluish grey or even a silvery tint. It seems that we used not differentiate between these colours when they were part of nature, realising that the colours are constantly shifting.

For anything non-natural that is green, one uses the word *uaine*. Only natural things can be referred to as *glas*, but there's quite a range of things that can be described as having this colour: tears, foreigners, ice, fog and naturally coloured wool.

One of the most common associations of the word *glas* is with Glas Gaibhleann, a mythic cow that provides an inexhaustible supply of milk. The *glas* in her name means both 'grey' and 'green'. She was a grey cow, forked with bolts of white (*gaibhleann* means 'white-loined' or 'forked'), but she could make any pasture she grazed greener and lusher. An especially verdant field was (and still is, occasionally) called a *glas gaibhleann*, in the belief that it had been grazed by this benevolent beast at night.

There are stories from every county about Glas Gaibhleann's adventures, and many are listed in the Schools Folklore Collection (1937), which gives details of the pastures she used to frequent. At one time most fields that were especially lush were attributed to her secret night-time grazing. If she seems familiar to you it is because she is most likely a reimagining of the pagan mother goddess Bó Finn, who nourished her people with endless milk. Mythological tropes such as these aren't something that new learners of Irish are generally aware of, though the tales of Glas Gaibhleann are an exception because they reflect our current environmental concerns.

From the myriad Glas Gaibhleann stories I'll choose just one, which was told by Frank O'Hare of Drumgoon, Co. Cavan. Before relating his tale he noted that his grandmother had told him of Glas Gaibhleann grazing each year on a plain along the River Annaghlee in the townland of Lisnagoon on 'the Green'. According to O'Hare's grandmother, the cow often complained that the land would become inaccessible because of little 'fields and narrow ridges'. (This seems to predict the arrival of the enclosures in the 19th century. These would take possession of the land that had been held in common for centuries.)

In the tale told by O'Hare this generous cow supplied all those in need with milk, readily filling up any vessel that was brought to her, until one greedy individual (typically portrayed as a witch) grew envious and made a bet with the local people that she could provide a vessel that the cow couldn't fill.

Next day the witch returned with a sieve, which she demanded that the cow fill. Glas Gaibhleann did her best and kept yielding milk but 'soon there was milk up to her hocks. She looked behind her and saw it flowing down across the fields and into the ditches.' Nevertheless, she kept on giving of herself, until eventually blood began to flow from her teats. She roared three times and all the calves she had had came running from afar. They gathered around her and, with one final plaintive cry, she and her calves turned clockwise once and disappeared from the land.

This is one of hundreds of similar accounts. The word used for Glas Gaibhleann's cry is often *diadhánach*, which you'll recall is the lonely bellowing of a cow bereft of her calf. The sound has a resonance and frequency that is unique. The story always stresses that Glas Gaibhleann was never seen again, though it is believed the marks of her hoofs or of a three-legged milking stool can still be seen on prominent local rocks.

THE ECOLOGY
OF IRISH

The Glas Gaibhleann story is a sobering parable of unsustainable agricultural practices, but it seems that it's not just a reappraisal of an ancient myth that has been repurposed for our contemporary environmental concerns. Its message was always about the dangers of exploiting limited resources and not caring for the land and animals. It's a reminder of how much environmental guidance is contained within the language.

Countless metaphors, similes and proverbs are based on natural phenomena, such as *An tráth a ghaireann an chuach ar an sceach lom, díol do bhó agus ceannaigh arbhar* ('When the cuckoo cries on the bare thorn bush, sell your cow and buy corn'), *An lao ite i mbolg na bó* ('The calf eaten in the belly of the cow') and *Gach éan mar a oiltear, agus an naosc san abar* ('Every bird as it is brought up, and the snipe in the mud').

Our connection to the natural world has degraded to the extent that it's hard to decipher the second and third proverbs. Yet they show how much the language is immersed in the landscape and even has a natural bias towards biodiversity and sustainability. This is most evident in the expression *An gobadán i mbeál cuaiche* ('The meadow pipit in the mouth of a cuckoo'), which predicts the chaos that will follow when the reliable conventions of nature are no longer dependable and go awry.

The meadow pipit raises the cuckoo's chicks. So, the large cuckoo depends on the little pipit for her survival. And if she is about to devour the pipit then things are not good for either the pipit or the cuckoo. The expression reminds us to be careful about destroying that which we need to survive.

Gobadán is the Irish name for a meadow pipit, though it can also mean sandpiper and sharp-tongued person. Depending on where in the country you are, a meadow pipit can also be *banaltra na cuaiche* ('cuckoo's nursemaid'), *riabhóg mhóna* ('little stripe of the peat'), *coimhdire na cuaiche* ('cuckoo's chaperone'), *fuiseog mhóna* ('turf lark'), *gobadán na cuaiche* ('cuckoo's sandpiper') or *caológ riabhach* ('little streak of the meadow'). There is one further name for meadow pipit, *cúlóg riabhach*, which is just a derivation of the latter, but it can also mean a bishop's secretary or a county councillor chasing after a politician, as both the secretary and the councillor mimic the meadow pipit's desperate fixation on following a cuckoo in flight.

The language delights in this diversity of terms for things that, to a city-dweller, may seem very similar. Remember the range of words to describe bestial rutting (*dáir* among cattle, *clíth* among swine, *eachmhairt* among horses, *snafach* among donkeys, *reith* among sheep, *imreas* among goats, *soidhir* among hounds, *láth* among deer and so on)? Well, there are even more words to describe different forms of salmon, from the well-known *bradán* to *éigne, toineamh, eithir, moghna, maighre* and *iach*. *Coraghiobach* is a male salmon, while *gruanach* is a male salmon in springtime. *Maighreán* is a small salmon, *gadluine* a salmon after spawning. *Liachóg* is a cross between a salmon and a trout, as is *colgán*. *Gilidín* is a salmon fry, as is *bláthán* and *gealóg*, though these three words can also refer to brown trout fry, as they are difficult to differentiate at that age. *Earc* can mean a speckled salmon, and *glasóg* is yet another kind of salmon.

There is a verb for the action of salmon making hollows in the sand of riverbanks to set her *saothar* ('spawn') in. That word is *clasaigh*, which can also be used for humans making furrows or trenches. And my favourite salmon word of all is *samhnachán*, which means a landlocked salmon or brown trout

– one that spends its life in a tidal estuary without heading out to sea to become an ocean salmon or sea trout or one that lingers in the estuary without coming back up through the river system to spawn. 'Slob trout' is probably the nearest English equivalent but there are significant differences.

Such words may seem like quaint vestiges now, but the danger is that when we cull descriptive terms for the world around us we narrow our ability to perceive its diversity. We lose touch with our surroundings, both physically and linguistically. Once the last person who understands the word *samhnachán* (or the Hiberno-English version, salmnahaun) dies, does the knowledge of what it refers to vanish with them?

Remember the word *diadhánach*, the lonely bellowing of a cow bereft of her calf? Before hearing that word I had never stopped to consider how the process of acquiring butter and cream from an animal depended on an amoral act: forcibly removing a cow, goat or sheep from her baby, violently breaking the bond of maternal love and care. I had never thought about how the roars of grief from a cow can continue for days. The sudden awareness of this altered my perception and changed me. Nowadays when I hear the lowing coming from a farmyard I can feel the anguish rising through me, sparked by the mother's despair and the strength of her desire to be reunited with her offspring.

Later, when I learnt the word *gnúsacht*, my awareness of this betrayal was further heightened, which led me to give up beef. *Gnúsacht* means the quiet under-lowing of a cow to her calf. It is the same loving, nurturing sound that any mother makes to her child. I had heard the sound before but had never thought about it until I learnt the word. It seems appropriate that *lacht* is one of many words for 'milk' in Irish, as it also means a gathering of tears, as if acknowledging how precious this liquid is.

Languages that are still rooted to these elemental processes help us contend with the natural alchemy behind the production of our food. They plug us back in to the animal and plant world that we are all drifting away from, and they also ignite a compassion for the beings we share the Earth with. We get to stop and consider whether it is right that hormone-rich nourishment that a mother lactates to feed her offspring should be exploited so that we can enjoy butter and lattés.

The old way of extracting milk by hand seemed to give the cow more honour; there was even a word to describe this streaming forth of milk from her teat, *comhthál*. The tál in this word refers to the act of yielding freely, also to flowing or springing forth, and the prefix comh acknowledges that it is being done with the compliance of the cow. The farmer or milkmaid cares for the cow, which willingly offers her milk in return. Irish mythology regarded cows as a gift from the gods to nourish us. We treated them with honour and they in turn nurtured us.

That the milking process was perhaps plea-surable to the cow is conveyed in the word *eadra*, which means a late morning milking after a spell of earlier grazing but also conveys a sense of the reassuringly satiated feeling that a cow experiences after she's filled her belly with grass in the morning and then instinctively wanders down towards the *buaille*, the field where the cows wait before being milked. Her udder is full and she's looking forward to the relief of having it emptied as the farmer or milkmaid tugs right down to the *sniogadh*, the last few – and the richest – drops in the teat. This sense has extended the meaning of *eadra* to refer to a bout of late-morning idle gossiping or loitering once the chores have been done. It conveys the idea of relaxation and an abundance of time.

The greater number of words like these in a language the more attuned we become to our relationship with animals. I learnt the phrase *cnead is duais* – the suffering of a cow immediately before death – at about the same time as learning *gnúsacht*, and it marked another point on my path towards vegetarianism. This was further strengthened by knowledge of the word *donáladh*, the frequent bellowing of a cow through pain.

Although the old way of milking was more intimate and humane, the degree to which we have always exploited cattle is well attested to by the number of words that refer to ways of hobbling them. We came on *buicmín* earlier, which is the piece of wood that fastens the spancel cord binding a cow's foreleg to her horn. There's also *speirsín*, a rope or cord fastened round the hock to impede her movements; *buaircín*, a piece of wood placed on the horns of a troublesome cow; *crann-nasc*, a kind of spancel that ties the horns to a foreleg; *dan*, a rope tied round the horns to prevent her jumping out of a canoe; and *buarach*, a rope to bind the hindlegs while she is being milked. The latter also means a trap.

The *buarach* was known as a *glúinineach* in Waterville, Co. Kerry, and as a *glaicín* in Kincasslagh and Gweedore, Co. Donegal. A spancel for the forelegs was known as a *rucall* when I was growing up in Corca Dhuibhne, and it was still being made from the hairs of a cow's tail until shortly before I was born. It was also known as an *urchall* or *airchomal*.

The images that these words evoke make you cheer for the existence of a *bó dhodach*, a cow that purposely spills her milk pail when it is full, and of a *bó bhradach*, which is a cow with wanderlust that will go to any lengths to break out and explore her area. Both character traits caused strife and expense to farmers, yet both were tolerated and even regarded with a degree of admiration, as far as I can recall from my youth.

Words like *diadhánach* and *donáladh* have a bell-like quality that makes us stop and think. They help define a specific element but also show how it is connected to its surroundings and ultimately to everything else in the universe, just as the chime of a bell radiates to an inaudible infinity in all directions.

That words like *gnúsacht* still exist allow us to get to know the interior of the exterior – of the human and animal world but also of the subterranean existence to all things. I've been nourished by these words and the insights they've given me.

COWS AND COPPER

I t's easy to underestimate just how bovine-centric
Irish is. The influence of cattle on words, expressions and ideas is profound. The Irish word for 'boy'
is *buachaill*, which also means 'cowherd', and the
word for road is *bóthar*, 'cow path'. (A wider road is
a *slige*, or *slí*, in Modern Irish; it was wide enough
for two ox-pulled carts to pass. The word derives
from the act of felling trees to clear a way.)

We've already seen how the name of the earth
goddess Bóinn is from *bó fhionn*, 'white cow', and

the Milky Way is Bealach na Bó Finne ('The Way of the White Cow'). And, of course, our central saga, Táin Bó Cuailnge, is all about cattle rustling.

This fixation on cattle all comes down to a genetic mutation that came with us to Ireland about four thousand years ago. It's a sequence of DNA on the MCM6 gene of chromosome 2. It gives us the ability to tolerate lactose in adulthood, and without it we would never become cow people fixated on milk and butter.

When analysing the DNA of skeletons in Ireland from five thousand years ago, scientists find no trace of this DNA sequence. Nor do these earlier inhabitants have any of the other genetic markers that are common to us. It seems that they are not our ancestors. We are not related to the first settlers or even to those who came after and built the great tombs of Newgrange and Loughcrew. At some point in the following thousand years we arrived here and brought with us cattle, cereals, ceramics and the mutation in our DNA. Certainly, our devotion to cattle has been evident since. One of our most important ancient manuscripts is Leabhar na hUidhre ('Book of the Dun Cow'), and our mythology is rich with tales of cows, like Glas Gaibhleann and Bó Riabhach ('Brindle Cow') who in the final year of her life boasted that she could survive through the winter and the cold spring months no matter how harsh the weather was. The month of March regarded this as a challenge and extended its dominance into the first three days of April, bringing with it storms that killed the old cow, then stripped her skin and bleached her bones. Even today, if the early days of April are inclement they are called *laethanta na Bó Riabhaí* ('days of the Brindle Cow').

Cattle and dairy metaphors are used to describe many aspects of nature. A ladybird is *bóín Dé* ('God's cow'), an old name for a cucumber is *lus na bó* ('cow's herb'), cowslip juice is *bainne bó bleachtáin* ('milk of a milch cow'), a child of bad parents is *lao bó bradaí* ('calf of a thieving or trespassing cow'). One of the finest blessings to bestow on a farmer is *Go mbeidh cac bó agat go deo*

('May you have cow dung for ever'), which is a way of acknowledging the nourishment and healthy micro-bacteria that a cow brings to a household. Among the most esteemed of herbal remedies was *fual bó* ('cow's urine'), considered the essence of all wildflowers, as opposed to *maothachán* and *steámar*, which refer to stale human urine, though this too was valued for use in the *soitheach bhéal easrach*, a urine tub for felting wool (literally, 'vessel with a trampling mouth').

There are many other intriguing cow words that oughtn't be overlooked, like *bearradóir*, a cow that eats the hair off her tail or other cows' tails. It also means one who probes for bogwood by means of an iron bar, or a detective. *Ablach* means 'plunder' or 'ransacking', such as that done by cows in a field of wheat. It can also mean a slovenly person, a glutton, a carcass or an overweight or inert person, and it also describes the sudden effort at catching an animal, like reaching to grab for a calf, and the way in which a dog might lurch at you.

Fíbín refers to the crazed buck-leaping a cow can suddenly resort to when being tormented by a gadfly laying eggs under her skin. Cattle have been known to hurl themselves over cliffs and drown themselves in lakes in their panic to avoid these flies. *Stropán* means a cow's afterbirth, as does *broghais*, though it also means a lazy or untidy person, a soiled or torn garment or any dirty, soft thing. *Bóithreán* means dried cow dung used as fuel, or dust on the road, or a languorous gait that might raise this dust.

But most relevant here is the word *carn-umha*, which is used to describe a cow's udder that has solid corners, as occasionally happens after calving. The word actually translates as 'copper heap', *umha* being the word used for copper possibly for eons, because the other key element we brought with us as well as our DNA mutation was knowledge of how to mine copper and transform it into bronze.

The insights we had into how to mix a small amount of tin or arsenic with copper that had been extracted from its ore to form *cré-umha*, bronze, led to our dominance on this island – or at least it did for those who favoured adding tin to the copper rather than arsenic (the latter tended to die off pretty quickly).

It was our skill in producing *cré-umha* and our domestication of cattle that made our language and culture usurp whoever and whatever was here before us. Our resilient bronze tools outmatched their stone axes, awls and flint blades, and we set about creating the landscape of today – a Burren denuded of trees for our cattle to graze in, a land free of bears that might endanger them, and long causeways, like Claí na Muice Duibhe (Black Pig's Dyke) in Cos. Monaghan and Leitrim, that spanned the country, possibly to keep livestock in or to drove them long distances across the wetlands.

Bronze keeps appearing in the early legal and religious tracts and sagas as *criad-umha*, *cri uma*, *crédumae*, but it was one particular line in the Brehon Law tracts (written down in the eighth century but dating from far earlier) that made me stop and think. It was *in t-uma fora claiter in aill* ('the copper for which the cliff is pierced').

I was in west Co. Cork when I first encountered it. In fact I was walking along the cliffs of Mizen Head, which are still streaked with strips of copper ore. Nearby, at Mount Gabriel, I could see the marks where our ancestors had pierced the rock to obtain the ore. Their mine shafts extending into the mountain are still charred from the fires they lit to extract this *umha* ('copper') to make *cré-umha* ('bronze').

I was reminded of Lubhdán, king of the fairies, whose voice was *gluair áib uma* ('clear and sweet as copper's resonance'). It was precisely this resonance that captured me – the ripples of culture and language tracing back through time. I've often stood in the National Museum in Dublin staring at the bronze axe-heads and spearheads and knives and razors – transfixed by these time-warp objects. It is said that they constitute only 0.2% of the 370 tonnes of copper that were extracted from the two principal copper mines of Mount Gabriel and Ross Island in Co. Kerry. The rest may have eroded and corroded, though it may still be hidden in hordes beneath the ground.

It makes me wonder whether words like *umha* also make up a similar tiny percentage of the language that was once spoken. Has 99.8% of it vanished? It's impossible to know for certain, though I do know that I can still walk into any hardware shop in the Gaeltacht today and ask for a strip of *umha ar a cumanuibh* ('copper for their hurling sticks'), which is a line from an ancient law tract concerning the seizure of property for the satisfaction of debt, and be understood.

The language allows us a closeness to those ancient times that is both uncanny and alluring.

CURSES

I t's surprising to have progressed this far without having addressed the subject of swearing and vocal vilification. As a mode of expression, cursing in Irish extends far beyond mere name-calling or petty insults. For a flavour of what's possible, try the following:

> Go n-ithe an chráin mhíolach thú. ('May the louse-infested sow eat you.')

Go mbí do chaolán amuigh agat. ('May your
small intestine be forced out of you.')

The Irish people are now renowned for their
skill in cursing in English, and this possibly stems
from the eagerness with which we used to issue
hexes and maledictions. Seeking revenge through
'backward blessings' or malicious magic was a
common practice, as can be seen from a cursory
glance at the old chronicles. The practice stemmed
primarily from our belief in the power of the word,
just as it did with the Egyptians in the times of
the Pharaohs, who cast destructive spells on those
who slighted them, using the powers of Heka, a
form of magic based on the ability of words to
influence reality. Over the years the power of Irish
mallachtaí ('curses') has shifted from manifesting
physical change in the world towards simply
causing dishonour.

Go dté do rabharta go mallmhuir ort. ('May
your high tide ebb to a neap tide.')

Go bhfana an bhuinneach choíche ort. ('May
you suffer from diarrhoea for ever.')

The language scolds, belittles and harangues
people by wishing hardship or misfortune on them,
or by summoning the devil, rather than simple
name-calling or petty insults. Rarely does an Irish
curse refer in uncouth terms to copulation or the
reproductive organs. Instead they assert their power
through summoning bad deeds and adversity.

Go mbí agat bean ghránna, ba bána agus tigh
ar ard. ('May you have an ugly wife, sterile
cattle and an exposed house.')

⌣

Srathair na hainnise ar chapall do thubaiste.
('The yoke of misfortune on your horse of
misery.')

In this way they derive more from folk magic,
charms and spells, like the *geiseanna* we encountered earlier. They are malicious, and at their most
extreme claim the power not only to dishonour but

to inflict actual harm. They can't easily be rescinded in the same way as you might apologise to someone you had simply sworn at conventionally.

> Go gcrochfar ard ar lá gaoithe thú. ('May you hang high on a windy day.')

⁓

> Cré na cille chugat. ('May the earth of the graveyard engulf you.')

A series of complicated steps must be taken before a curse can be lifted, involving such things as seeking the services of a wise woman or witch doctor, felling a piece of hawthorn and striking the ground with it or doing some other act of reparation.

We've already seen that the poet and druid could issue utterances that not only undermine a person's honour but that had a tangible impact; like the way that Aodhagán Ó Rathaille could suppos- edly raise a welt on a person's face with one of his *aortha* ('satires'). Other, lesser poets were capable of *rannaireacht* ('rhyming'), which, done right, were almost as powerful.

Senchán, the chief poet in the seventh century, managed to rhyme the mice of Guaire's palace to death with a satirical verse when they ate his leftovers after a feast. He had learnt the skill from a *toirpéist* ('great monster') that he encountered on a road in Scotland. Senchán 'conversed with him in the obscurity of poetry', hence his nickname, Senchán Toirpéist.

We've also seen that words were just as capable of doing good, as with the healing charms that were believed to banish illness by their mere utterance. *Briocht* is a word for a positive incantation, and also for a legend cut on the blade of a weapon.

> *Saol gadhair agus sláinte an bhradáin chugat*
> *– croí folláin agus gob fliuch* ('A dog's life and
> the salmon's health to you – healthy heart
> and wet mouth.')

Cursing in Irish is, certainly, very different from cursing in English, most noticeably in the fact that it doesn't rely on terms for sexual reproduction. As a result, the words relating to copulation are far less offensive and have fewer taboos surrounding them than in English. This is why they are used quite openly among people in the Gaeltacht, although it is done only among themselves and mostly between members of the same sex. That said, there are some curses that are vulgar.

Clúmh ar do pholl. ('Hair on your anus.')

———

Míola id chraiceann is gearb ar do ghabhal.
('Lice on your skin and scabs on your crotch.')

The scholar and translator Robin Flower wrote of being cursed at by the renowned storyteller Peig Sayers on the Blasket Islands at some point in the 1930s. She banished him from her cottage, saying, 'The devil eat you between the earth and sky.' At least, this was how he translated what she had said in Irish. He was taken aback but she later explained that he shouldn't have been concerned. He translated her explanation as:

If the curses come from the heart, it would be
a sin. But it is from the lips they come, and
we use them only to give force to our speech ...

The problem is that you never know if they are
coming from the heart or not. Certainly if you hear
a curse summoning the devil, you should take heed,
although his power is receding as fewer and fewer
people believe in him.

Go stróice an diabhal thú. ('May the devil
shred you.')

—

Go ndéana an diabhal dréimire de cnámh
do dhroma. ('May the devil make a ladder of
your backbone.')

—

Go n-ithe an cat thú, is go n-ithe an diabhal
an cat. ('May the cat eat you, and may the
devil eat the cat.')

If you need a truly powerful insult it is worth
reaching back to Old Irish, even though few will

understand you. It may take a while for modern speakers to work it out, so that it becomes a slow-release insult, only gradually releasing its venom.

Uí airim brocshalaig. ('You grandson of a ploughman, filthy like a badger.')

—

A ulcha gaillín detbudánaig cúarlúpánaig. ('You comb of a castrated cockerel, smoky-coloured, bent and crooked.')

—

Mac ro boí oc gaillsig goit grúcbuirr. ('You son of a stammering, surly, puffed-up foreign woman.')

—

Adarc bó rodraige. ('You horn of an infertile cow.')

These are just some of the many thousands of curses waiting to be discovered. If you need one for a particular situation, as with everything else, there's now an app for that. It's been devised by the scholar Dennis King and is hosted on the website of Sabhal Mòr Ostaig, Scotland's National Centre for Gaelic Language and Culture on the Isle of Skye. The app can help generate updated curses in Modern Irish for, say, 'May an enormous puffball destroy your hard drive.' There's a separate curse generator for Old Irish, which can translate phrases like 'May you meet a goat-headed monster that will defile your hard cheese / woad garden / tuberous root.'

ILLUSION

Maybe the best way to think about languages is as the compound eye of a dragonfly, which sees through thousands of lenses at once, combining them into a single image. This is ultimately what words attempt to do and old languages in particular have a range and field-width to their lenses that offer greater perspectives and more unusual angles, allowing us to see underworlds and other realms.

Some of the terms I have discussed so far may have sparked certain things – memories, awareness, emotion or a sudden *spailp* ('spark', 'surprise kiss') of insight, the like of which occasionally arises when folk memories that linger in the deepest recesses of our minds are triggered. It's hard to define or categorise these things. They arise from a non-rational cellular awareness, or they arise because the brain works in a mysterious, multidirectional way, so that everything is linked to everything else. It's the antithesis of the prevailing linear, logical and sequential thinking.

In fact we are a momentous tangle of intangible interconnections, with every neuron linked to as many as ten thousand others. It is this interconnectivity that elicits these unaccountable and untranslatable sensations, intuitions and feelings, which appear and then disappear at the edge of consciousness.

Irish seems to work more on this level than other modern languages. Some of its older and odder words poke at the embers of old fires we thought had died out – possibly because, as we've seen, the language is based on an awareness that sound is an energy – a vibration capable of carrying and transferring information within it.

I like to think of it in terms of the *duirling*, the springtide mark on the shore where the waves strike the stones only indirectly by shifting the underlying sand or by hurling stones that in turn hit other stones in a complex game of coastal billiards. Each stone may think it is its own entity, but in fact it doesn't exist in its present location or form without the tide. They are as intertwined as people are to their parents.

This is how words operate within a language, yet we also need to be able to differentiate each word so that we can employ them as tools to perform different functions. For example, the word *cloch* ('stone') summons an image of a solid lump of minerals. On another level our brain realises that there is no such thing as a stone – that beneath the level of cellular structure there are just particles, pulsating as waves. At that level everything is one, and the only way the brain can arrange this infinite particle soup of oneness into a comprehensible reality is by thinking in terms of holographs.

That's what we do when we hear a word like *cloch*. Our mind summons an internal holograph of it, and with a language that has such a variety of terms for stone, the mind becomes nimble at summoning more specific images.

Yet the reverse can also be true. The principal word, *cloch*, can be stretched to encompass a range of things, including a pebble, whetstone, millstone, corner stone, anchor stone, gallstone, cherry stone and coping stone, and also a testicle, a rocky island, an old castle and a stony shore. There are, of course, words for each of these, but *cloch* suffices once the context is clear.

It's all somewhat bamboozling but also strangely liberating. That consciousness has learnt to create and then project a stable image based on this bewildering muddle is inspiring. It's a conjuring act that we succumb to each and every minute, and the language then needs to keep pace with this.

For me the word *eascair* helps clarify all this. It means to summon up or sprout or leap into being. It can also mean to emerge from the loins of one's ancestors or to rise from the ground like a tree, or to emerge from a plant like an ear of corn. This latter sense has extended its meaning to a grain of corn or a kernel. *Eascair* conveys the idea of manifestation, of rising from the oneness into a seemingly separate form. It's how we emerged and how our language works, so maybe it's no wonder that it's also how reality is formed.

The idea of our reality being make-believe, or a holographic illusion, is hinted at by the word *ciall*, which means 'sense', 'meaning', 'intellect', 'reason', 'wisdom' or 'knowledge'; but then, as if to suggest that the opposite is also the case, the phrase *cur i gcéill* means to pretend or to fool someone.

The idea of imagining and manifesting holographic realities from a sea of quantum wave particles, or of summoning things out of nothing, is not too far from how a druid would have regarded the ability to manifest and mould reality. There's an understanding of this still in the verb *nochtaim*, meaning 'I declare' or 'I disclose' something but also to manifest this or bring it to light, as though these elements could be connected. Vocalising something helps brings it into reality or into the hologram of our consciousness. *Nochtaim* can also mean 'I unsheathe a sword' or 'I undress a body'.

This idea of summoning matter by pulling it out of the ether is also hinted at in the word *léir*, which means 'visible', 'manifest' and 'clear' but also 'destruction', 'ruin' and 'woe', as though acknowledging that making things solid or visible in this dimension is a temporary act that invariably leads to their eventual ruin.

We often encounter this paradox, whereby things that look separate are in fact intertwined, such as how the word *tonn* means both a single wave and the entire ocean, or how *cos* means 'foot' and 'leg' (because there cannot be a foot without a leg). We need only adjust our gaze to realise that everything is unified.

Perhaps the idea of the individual and the communal being connected by the interactions between them has become harder to grasp as society has shifted towards the individual view. Yet the aim of language has always been to bridge these gaps between people, to transcend our isolation and reinforce our connection with one another and with our surroundings. Language develops and strengthens our interrelatedness with all life and reveals our empathy and the dependence we have on each other and on our world.

Whether we regard ourselves as sea waves or shore stones greatly affects our perspective on the world, yet they are ultimately the same. Both reveal that we are one while being many.

A COLLECTION
OF FISH

So, finally, what can be said to summarise the scattershot of words I have presented? We must first bear in mind that to fully appreciate any of these words – to grasp the array of processes beneath their surface and their ability to convey more than merely rational ideas – we need to encounter them within the biosphere of a thriving Gaeltacht. Here, on these pages, they have been unceremoniously plucked from their natural habitat and brought spluttering into the awkward medium of black lines on a white background.

Yet my hope is that some of their complexity has been unravelled and that we have developed a sense that words can offer glimpses into the interior of the exterior of life in Ireland – not only of the human experience but of the indescribable, and often indecipherable, energies and activities taking place beneath the surface and behind the veil.

Old languages are like the bellows of an accordion, each word folding out to create maps, diagrams and sonic impressions that stretch back through time. By compressing these folds, memories and meanings are released in the form of audible notes that resonate with rapport for those that went before them.

The key thing to grasp from this *rothán* of words (*rothán* means a hank of fish, berries, mushrooms and so on threaded together on string or on a stem of grass) is that they reveal that we used to believe profoundly in the power of thought to influence life. Feeling something or becoming conscious of it could help manifest it, and this concept is behind many Irish words, such as *mothaím*, which means 'I feel' but also 'I become conscious of' or 'I awake'. Yet its older and truer meaning is 'I bewitch' or 'I practise magic on'. It's a good example of the belief that thinking is the basis of all reality, much as it still is in Buddhism or in the creative visualisation practices of New Age mysticism.

Every word rings out with the notion that we are creators connected to a panoply of gods and beings that may still exist between the rocks, beneath the seas and inside the trees. They have within them an implicit awareness that human beings are consequential and have agency. Ultimately, what old languages communicate most clearly is that we are far more than biddable drones or clones to be sold things to: we are independent beings with our own dreams, motivations and power.

At our best we are capable of manifesting entire realities, not just from our actions but from our thoughts and our words. There may be seven billion of us but each is as central to existence as the other.

I'd go so far as to say that a word like *cáithnín* (which you'll remember means a tiny speck of flour, a subatomic particle, a husk of corn or goosebumps) can lead us to an awareness of how we are an indefinable, uncategorisable confluence of forces – a fascinatingly fragmented array of thoughts, feelings, senses, intuitions and aspirations as interrelated to the rest of existence as a raindrop, despite how separate we might feel. Ideas like this help remind me that I am rooted to this world at an elemental level and that this life is mine to create.

I realise that some readers will have baulked at my overemphasis on the mythic and magical dimensions of the language and that such ideas are increasingly hard for people to swallow. But as the language itself makes clear, this was a central component of our understanding of the world for a long time. The poet Nuala Ní Dhomhnaill highlights this in her account of how her aunt would often respond to a knock on the door with the words

An de bheoaibh nó de mhairbh thú? ('Are you of the living or of the dead?'). Ní Dhomhnaill has also recalled coming across a drawer in the index of the Folklore Commission in University College, Dublin, titled *Neacha neamhbeo agus nithe nach bhfuil ann* ('Non-living beings and things that don't exist').

The mystical has been central to the lives of people for so long that we ought at least to remain open to the possibility that such thoughts have merit. The problems we now face in society, whether educational, environmental or systemic, will require us to rely on all facets of our experience and perception – and we should consider employing our mythical and spiritual capacities, as well as our more conventional sensory-based intellect, rather than relegating it all to the spheres of religion and philosophy.

Life is certainly dense with levels of experience, both mainstream and liminal, and I hope that this book has shown that Irish can be one way to access some of its overlooked layers. When we dare to tune in, or open up to it, certain things begin to show themselves. Maybe they do so gently to begin with, but over time the invisible and inaudible become visible and audible, and our lives are deepened and enriched.

———

Finally, I should say something about the demise of Irish, with so many of the words I have listed now extinct or on the path towards it. For example, the word *rothán* I used above to mean a collection of things to be threaded has other meanings that I am compelled to include. It can also mean a tether clasp that moves freely in a groove, a twisted band of rushes to hold the whorl of a spinning-wheel, a loop of hair twisted and plaited, or a volume of forcefully uttered words or imprecations.

Despite the listings of words in peril, this book should not be taken as an elegy or a wake. Rather, my hope was to summon forth a *hurlamaboc* ('rambunctious celebration') or a bout of *cíle-má-guairle* or *liútar-éatar*, *ruaille-buaille* or *ciara-má-boc*, which all mean much the same thing. I've simply tried to trace and chase the tails of things, the tail end of tales and truths – and whatever insights that lie in between.

I am not despairing about the gradual fading of the richness of the language, because Irish is as much a story as a language, and most stories never really die. Even if they are not retold every day, they linger in the depths of our mind. Every speaker is a narrator of this epic tale, and every word carries within it a piece of the plot. Every word also has extra layers of wisdom and insight encoded in it that allow us to delve deeper into the psyche and landscape of this island. We can still protect and keep alive the essence and wisdom contained in the language, even if many of the old words do what all words eventually do, which is to adapt, mutate or die off.

Let's end with a blessing to send us on our way. It protects against a swathe of ailments. Legend has it that it was first said by St Gall in the sixth or seventh century, but it is clearly far older than that.

Tessurc marb bíu. Ar díring, ar goth-sring,
ar att díchinn, ar fuilib híairn, ar ul loscas

tene, ar ub hithes cú. Rop achuh rú, crinas teoracnoe, crete teoraféthe fichte, benim a galar ar fiuch fuili guil Fuil nirub att rée rop slán.

———

'I save the dead-alive. Against belching, against javelin cord, against unkind swelling, against iron wounds, against an edge fire-burned, against a point that a dog bites. Let him be sharply red, three nuts withering, believe that three sinews are woven. I strike his illness, I overcome wounds lamenting of blood. Let it not be an endless swelling. Let him be healthy.'

REFERENCES

For the past three years I've been travelling around Ireland performing a show called *Arán & Im* ('Bread & Butter') in which I bake sourdough bread and discuss Irish words while the audience churns butter. I am often asked if there is a printed source where people can find all the words I use. Alas, there is not. In 2020 I spent two months roaming the coastal roads of Donegal, Sligo and Mayo gathering sea words and maritime terms for a performance called *Sea Tamagotchi*, and again, while few of these words were collated anywhere, I've now recorded them on www.manchan.com. But there are certain publications and websites that contain a rich compendium of interesting words and that I relied heavily on in compiling this book.

The preeminent one is the Irish–English dictionary compiled by Father Patrick Dinneen. A PDF version of the *Pocket Irish–English Dictionary* (1904) can be found online. The full dictionary was published in 1927. It too is available online, in Irish type. It's in searchable form on a University of Limerick website and can be 'borrowed' in digital format from Internet Archive. Hard copies are available from the Irish Texts Society.

Liam S. Gogan was commissioned to compile an updated Irish–English Dictionary in the 1950s. It was never published but it can be searched online at focloir.com. Another pioneering lexicographer was T. O'Neill Lane whose *Lane's English–Irish Dictionary* (1904) is online, as is his updated version, which is one and a half times larger: *Larger English–Irish Dictionary* (1915).

Other sources I relied on include Nuala Ní Dhomhnaill's *Selected Essays* (New Island, 2005) and Dennis King's blog posts on Old and Middle Irish at nimill.blogspot.com. For Old and Middle Irish I also consulted the vast store of knowledge in the Royal Irish Academy's online Dictionary of the Irish Language, at dil.ie. I did not consult Seán Ó Tuathail's *Foclóir Draíochta* (Dictionary of Druidism), but it might be of interest too.

The triumvirate of interconnected websites that present the latest research into place names (logainm.ie), folklore (dúchas.ie) and terminology (téarma.ie) have been invaluable, as have the digitised copies of more modern dictionaries, found at focloir.ie, teanglann.ie and potafocal.com.

Terence Patrick Dolan's *Dictionary of Hiberno-English* (3rd ed.) (Gill & Macmillan, 2012) is another wonderful treasure, as are various books by the amiable scholar of Hiberno-English Diarmuid Ó Muirthile, including *A Dictionary of Anglo-Irish* (Four Courts Press, 2000), *Words We Don't Use (Much Anymore)* (Gill & Macmillan, 2011) and

A Word in Your Ear (Four Courts Press, 1997).

Some of the words in the chapter on sexual terms are from Bishop John O'Brien's *Focalóir Gaoidhilge-Sax-Bhéarla* ('Dictionary of Irish-Saxon-English'), which was published in 1768 and is available online. A few unusual terms scattered throughout the book were gleaned from Father Allan MacDonald's *Gaelic Words and Expressions from South Uist and Eriskay* (Dublin Institute for Advanced Studies, 1958).

These books and myriad random articles from back issues of the Royal Irish Academy's journal, *Ériu*, and of the journal *Béaloideas*, published by the Folklore of Ireland Society, have acted as my *meitheal mhustrúin*, which means a gathering of people collected by an idle braggart to do work that he could have done himself.

Almost all the passages I've quoted from are available online. I adapted the translation of *The Song of Amergin* from R.A. Macalister's version. His original can be found in the translated text of *Lebor Gabála Érenn*, available on archive.org. I've quoted from two different translations of the Táin Bó Cúalgne; one edited and translated in 1898 by Eleanor Hull (from *The Cuchullin saga in Irish literature*, which can also be viewed on archive. org) and the other by my cousin Cecile O'Rahilly in 1967 (available on UCC's Corpus of Electronic Texts (CELT) website – celt.ucc.ie). The quotation from 'The Destruction of Da Derga's Hostel' is from Whitley Stokes's translation for *Revue Celtique* (1901) (available on celt.ucc.ie). I also quoted from Stokes's translation of 'The Hostel of Da Choca' (archive.org).

I've referenced three examples of early Irish poetry, two were from translations published by Eleanor Hull. One was from *Irish Gaelic Poetry into English Prose* (1912) and the other from *The Poem-Book of the Gael* (1912), both available on archive. org. The third was a poem translated by Gerard Murphy in *Early Irish Lyrics: Eighth to Twelfth Century* (1956). This book is not available online, but original Irish versions of the poems are at CODECS, the online database for Celtic Studies (vanhamel.nl/codecs).

There are many great translations of 'An Cailleach Bhéarra' to savour online. The version I chose was by the poet Anthony Weir, which he titles, 'The Earth Mother's Lamentation' (1975). Brian Merriman's 'Cúirt an Mheán Oíche' ('The Midnight Court') has also attracted a range of lively English renditions. I based the lines I've quoted on one by Noel Fahey, available at midnight-court.com.

I should make it clear that I am no scholar of the language or of linguistics, or of anything for that matter, despite having obtained a degree in Irish from University College, Dublin, three decades ago. This should be borne in mind as you decide how much credence to give anything I say. Irish-language scholarship is a notoriously elusive and contested discipline, and I've probably taken leaps and liberties that few experts would feel entirely comfortable with. To get a sense of quite how evanescent the study of Irish can be, consider that the word for 'etymology' is *sanasaíocht*, which derives from *sanas*, which means a whisper, a suggestion or a secret. It also means occult knowledge.

Three of the greatest 20th-century scholars of Irish – Myles Dillon, Brian Ó Cuív and David Greene – once had a lengthy and inconclusive discussion of how to say 'two cows' in Old Irish. Greene later remarked, 'If the three of us don't know, the chances are nobody knows.'

Since Modern Irish is an amalgamation of dialects, most of which were never written down, there can be no definitive account of any word. There was no standardised form for the majority of the population who were illiterate until the mid-20th century, and even then it was never fully adopted by all Gaeltacht regions. Therefore, there will always be other versions and spellings of any word you choose to mention. As Myles Dillon was known to comment, 'Nobody knows Irish.'

The best I can advise is to gauge for yourself what feels true in this book and dismiss anything that seems far-fetched or outlandish.